Teaching Cues for Basic Sport Skills for Elementary and Middle School Students

Hilda Fronske

and

Rolayne Wilson

Utah State University

Benjamin Cummings

Boston   San Francisco   New York
Capetown   Hong Kong   London   Madrid   Mexico City
Montreal   Munich   Paris   Singapore   Sydney   Tokyo   Toronto

Editor-in-Chief: Paul A. Smith
Editorial Assistant: Annemarie Kennedy
Editorial-Production Administrator: Deborah Brown
Editorial-Production Service: Colophon
Composition Buyer: Linda Cox
Manufacturing Buyer: Suzanne Lareau
Cover Administrator: Kristina Mose-Libon
Text Design and Composition: Publishers' Design and Production Services, Inc.
Photographer: Cherianne Mecham

Library of Congress Cataloging-in-Publication Data

Fronske, Hilda Ann.
    Teaching cues for basic sport skills for elementary and middle school students /
Hilda Fronske and Rolayne Wilson.
      p. cm.
    Includes bibliographical references and index.
    ISBN 0–205–30956–9 (alk. paper)
    1. Sports for children—Study and teaching.   2. Coaching (Athletics).
I. Wilson, Rolayne. II. Title.

GV361.F66   2002
796'.07'7—dc21   2001018900

Benjamin
Cummings

12345678910   0605040302
www.aw.com/bc

To my father and mother, who love children. Thank you for teaching me a great work ethic and for your love and belief in me. To our physical education professionals here at Utah State University. You're the best.

Hilda Fronske

To my parents, family, and friends. Thanks for your support, encouragement, and unconditional love. To the dedicated physical education professionals and students who have touched my life during my journey as a student and teacher

Rolayne Wilson

Preface

Have you ever dreamed of a book that would cover teaching cues, drill progressions, and mini-games for a variety of sport skills and activities for elementary and middle school students? The wait is over! Featured in this unique and exciting book are teaching cues for locomotor skills, manipulative skills, rope jumping, sprinting drills, Quad Ball, BMX cycling, in-line skating, recreational running, swimming, and soccer, just to name a few.

This book features live-action pictures of age-appropriate students executing the cues. This book also will save you hours of planning time by providing you with a user-friendly format. The cues will establish credibility with your students faster because you can tell them *why* a particular cue works.

ACKNOWLEDGMENTS

We thank Cherianne Mecham and Erin Van Langeveld for the great photographs, hard work, and their dedication to add "class" to the book. Thank you to Analisa Anderson, physical education teacher at Edith Bowen Laboratory School, for her willingness to share ideas, time, talent, and her students.

We thank Allyn and Bacon, including our editor, Joseph E. Burns, for his insight and another opportunity to publish; Deborah Brown, for her vision and expertise with the photos; and Annemarie Kennedy, for her time and patience with our questions.

We also wish to thank our reviewer Ann Smith, Chadron State College.

Our thanks to all the children who posed for the photos and for their talent and ability to perform many sport skills including Samantha Veibell, Kelcee Smith, Raysha Gladfelder, James Hortin, and McKade Brady. Special thanks to John and Cristina Hortin for their talent and participation in our photo shoot and to their parents, Sherilynn and John, for their effort and time. Thanks as well to the Edith Bowen Laboratory School—the students and Khaye Rhees, the principal.

We thank Dr. Art Jones, Debbie Tidwell, Jennifer Holt, and Beth Allen for their support and assistance with the book.

We thank Ralph and Marlene Meikle for their support and friendship.

We wish to thank all of the sport consultants who generously shared their time, knowledge, and expertise in their specific sport.

Teaching Physical Education Is Fun with the Right Tools: Analisa Anderson, elementary physical education specialist, Edith Bowen Laboratory School, Utah State University, Logan.

Locomotor Skills: Analisa Anderson, elementary physical education specialist, Edith Bowen Laboratory School, Utah State University, Logan.

Manipulative Skills: Analisa Anderson, elementary physical education specialist, Edith Bowen Laboratory School, Utah State University, Logan.

Rope Jumping: Don Disney and Caroline Disney, Heart Beat Enterprises, Columbia, Maryland.

Dynamic Stretches and Pillar Exercises: Jamie Hall/Bennion, USATF Track and Field Level 2 coach; head track coach, Mountain Crest High School, Hyrum, Utah; and graduate student assistantship, Utah State University, Logan.

Advanced Cues for Locomotor Skills: Jamie Hall/Bennion, USATF Track and Field Level 2 coach; head track coach, Mountain Crest High School, Hyrum, Utah; and graduate student assistantship, Utah State University, Logan.

Advanced Cues for Sprinting: Jamie Hall/Bennion, USATF Track and Field Level 2 coach; head track coach, Mountain Crest High School, Hyrum, Utah; and graduate student assistantship, Utah State University, Logan. Curtis Collier, track technician, Utah State University, Logan.

Basketball: Al Brown, assistant basketball coach for the Lady Volunteers, University of Tennessee, Knoxville; John Kras, assistant professor in physical education, Utah State University, Logan; Shanna Stevens, physical education major, Utah State University club basketball coach, Utah State University, Logan.

Floor Hockey: Ross Keys, physical education major, Utah State University, Logan; Michael Burggraf, physical education major, Utah State University, Logan.

Football: Jeff Berg, football player, Utah State University, Logan; Bill Bauer, Utah State University, Logan; Art Erickson, physical education teacher and head football coach, Mountain Crest High School, Hyrum, Utah.

Quad Ball: Joyce Harrison, professor, Brigham Young University, Provo, Utah.

Racquet Sports: Pickle-Ball/Tennis: Sarah Lowe, Angela Kimball, Amy Thatcher, and Jackie Ellis, tennis team at Utah State University, Logan; Tedi Searle, physical education major, Utah State University, Logan; Doug Smith, general manager, Pickle-Ball, Inc., Seattle, Washington.

Softball: Nicole Downs and Kelly Warner, physical education majors, Utah State University, Logan.

Soccer: Kelly Parsons, physical education major, Utah State University, Logan.

Track and Field: Jamie Hall/Bennion, USATF Track and Field Level 2 coach; head track coach, Mountain Crest High School, Hyrum, Utah; and graduate student assistantship, Utah State University, Logan; and Curtis Collier, track technician, Utah State University, Logan.

Volleyball: Launa Moser, head volleyball coach and teacher, Preston High School, Preston, Idaho; Carl McGown, head men's volleyball coach, Brigham Young University, Provo, Utah.

Ultimate Frisbee: Ann Asbell, activity specialist, Department of Exercise and Sport Science, Oregon State University, Corvallis; Janenne Graff, player/coach, Ultimate Frisbee Club, Utah State University, Logan; Jeremiah Yates, physical education major, Utah State University, Logan; Debbie Wilson, elementary physical education specialist, Oakwood Elementary School, Preston, Idaho.

Cycling: Tommy Murphy, physical education major, Utah State University, Logan; Jeff Keller, Sunrise Cycle, Logan, Utah; and Steven G. Gudmundson, Idaho Falls, Idaho.

In-Line Skating: Lisa Klarich Davis, physical education teacher, Ecker Hill Middle School, Park City, Utah; Margot Willett, program director, Skate in School, Edina, Minnesota.

Recreational Running: Debbie Wilson, elementary physical education specialist, Oakwood Elementary School, Preston, Idaho; Patrick Shane, head women's cross country/distance coach, Brigham Young University, Provo, Utah.

Swimming: Katrina Bingham, swimming and water aerobics instructor, Utah State University, Logan; Lisa Klarich-Davis, physical education teacher, Ecker Hill Middle School, Park City, Utah.

Contents

Preface   **v**

SECTION 1   INTRODUCTION

CHAPTER 1   Teaching Physical Education Is Fun with the Right Tools   1

SECTION 2   (GRADES K–3) FUNDAMENTAL SPORT SKILLS

CHAPTER 2   Locomotor (Traveling) Skills   19

CHAPTER 3   Throwing, Catching, and Kicking (Stationary)   29

SECTION 3   (GRADES K–8) ROPE JUMPING

CHAPTER 4   Learning the Ropes   39

SECTION 4   (GRADES 4–8) FUNDAMENTAL SPORT SKILLS

CHAPTER 5   Advanced Cues for Locomotor Skills   51

CHAPTER 6   Dynamic Stretching and Pillar Exercises   59

CHAPTER 7   Sprinting Drills   67

CHAPTER 8   Throwing, Catching, Striking, and Kicking   77

SECTION 5   **(GRADES 4–8) SPORTS**

CHAPTER 9   Basketball   91

CHAPTER 10   Floor Hockey   115

CHAPTER 11   Football   125

CHAPTER 12   Quad Ball   137

CHAPTER 13   Racquet Sports: Tennis and Pickle-Ball   151

CHAPTER 14   Soccer   169

CHAPTER 15   Softball, Slow-Pitch   185

CHAPTER 16   Track and Field   197

CHAPTER 17   Ultimate Frisbee   207

CHAPTER 18   Volleyball   217

SECTION 6   **LIFETIME ACTIVITIES**

CHAPTER 19   Cycling and BMX Riding   233

CHAPTER 20   In-Line Skating   247

CHAPTER 21   Recreational Running   257

CHAPTER 22   Swimming and Diving   267

            Index   **283**

rule, is that no one talks when a student or teacher is "on stage." Ask each student to stand and talk about something they enjoy playing, something they carry with them each day, or perhaps some piece of sports equipment they would like to be. Why is this activity critical on the first day? It "breaks the ice" between the students and the teacher. The students begin to feel comfortable with each other. They begin relating to each other's experiences. First impressions and judgements—good or bad—are replaced by feelings of warmth for the individual. The students feel more comfortable talking with each other, and they learn specific facts about their classmates. They can use this information to open a conversation. Walls come down. Relationships start to form. The teacher also benefits and has information with which to spark a later conversation.

Another reason this activity is so effective is that all students must be quiet. This teaches respect for each other, and the teacher can begin to work on management skills, which sets the tone for the rest of the year.

On the second day, have students network with a partner for about 5 minutes. Each student stands with the partner, and they share what they have learned about each other. Once again, emphasize the rule that no one else is to talk when partners are sharing their experiences about their new friend. Respect is reinforced. You will be amazed at how well the students listen during this time. Perform this type of activity throughout the year whenever you feel a need to bond with your class. The benefits of a supportive climate (Griffin & Patton, 1981) include the following:

- Group members accept more easily other's influence.
- Members of the group are less suspicious of the motives of others.
- A greater degree of tolerance of deviant behavior occurs.
- When conflicts arise, the group is able to focus on group goals rather than on defending egos.
- The group develops trust, which allows more freedom for group risk taking.
- Members of the group feel better about themselves.

Remember, the first few days are critical in terms of what you will do the rest of the year.

Supportive Climate Needed When Teaching Sport Skills

Teachers need to establish a framework of support in order to implement teaching cues successfully. Students need to feel safe in order to reach out and try new behaviors. Creating a supportive climate creates a safe learning environment for students. The supportive climate happens verbally, with positive, clear cues and reinforcing phrases. It also happens in a safe, nonverbal physical environment.

Nonverbal behaviors, which accompany verbal cues, also communicate to students. A teacher who says, "Nice dive," accompanied by a harsh tone of voice and disapproving facial expression, communicates "Bad dive." The way teachers present cues—the tone of their voices, their body language, their manner of touch, or dress (such as teacher not wearing a swimming suit)—can enhance or detract from a positive environment.

Figure 1.7   Building Relationships

Great teachers and coaches are skillful at giving the most appropriate cue at the appropriate time, using verbal and/or nonverbal signals. Combining verbal cues and positive nonverbal cues becomes a powerful tool for providing feedback from the teacher. By creating a supportive climate, you can help students feel comfortable and become motivated to explore and learn a variety of sports.

Build Relationships and Still Get the Work Done

How does a teacher continue to build relationships (Figure 1.7) and still get the work done? Theodore Roosevelt knew (as all leaders know) that "the royal road to a person's heart is to talk about the things he or she treasures most" (Carnegie, 1981, p. 94). Teachers have many opportunities to learn each day about students' lives and what they treasure. Here are some options to think about: Take time before school, at lunch, during recess, and after school to visit with your students. Interview them about their interests, dreams, and goals. Attend school functions to let them know you care about them. Let them talk about what they did over the weekend, on spring break, or during their summer vacations.

Expending the effort to build relationships with your students develops their respect and trust. They will be more willing to work for you, so work on building relationships daily. The best teachers do, and the work gets done in a supportive climate.

Protocols and Management Skills

Protocols are necessary to provide a safe learning environment and to provide structure for your students. Just like any sport skill, the protocols need to be practiced repeatedly. For further information, refer to Graham, Holt/Hale, and Parker (2000) and Pangrazi (2001). The following protocols are just a few to get you started:

1. Establish start and stop signals. The signals need to be different from each other. They can be auditory or visual, or a combination of both. For example, one whistle blow to start and two whistle blows to stop.

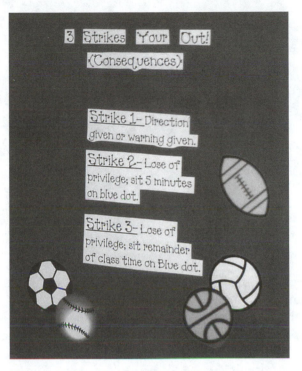

Figure 1.8   Protocols for Off-Task Behavior: Strike 1–Direction given or warning given; Strike 2–Loss of privilege, sit 5 minutes on blue dot; Strike 3–Loss of privilege; sit remainder of class time on blue dot.

2. Establish protocols for:
   - Entering and exiting the gym
   - A gathering place for giving instruction and talking to the entire class
   - Distributing and collecting of equipment
   - Grouping students: partners, small groups, teams, and so forth.
   - Off-task behavior. For example, three strikes, you're out—one strike is a warning; second strike, the student sits out for 5 minutes and observes the class; third strike, the student sits out the entire class (Figure 1.8).
3. Provide a piece of developmentally appropriate equipment for each student; this is key so students have many opportunities to practice sport skills. Teachers need to be creative in finding ways to work their budget to buy safe, age-appropriate equipment. For example, good, inexpensive leather volleyballs can be purchased from high school volleyball teams. Old tennis balls can be purchased from tennis teams or tennis clubs. Send home a letter with students at the beginning of the school year, indicating your equipment needs. Enlist the help of the high school shop or an applied technology school to make equipment. The Parent–Teacher Organization (PTO) may be able to provide funds. Use your creativity to find solutions (Figure 1.9).
4. Establish a "home" for the equipment when giving directions: for example, a basketball between the feet, standing inside of a hula hoop, bean bag on the floor (Figure 1.10).
5. Move around the perimeter of the area, with your back to the wall. You can observe the entire class, give instruction, and offer feedback to students.

Figure 1.9   Everyone Has a Piece of Equipment

6. Maximize activity time and minimize wait time. Mini-games are very effective in increasing OTRs and minimizing wait time.
7. Avoid having lines of students waiting for their turn.
8. Use caution about circle formations. See Wood's and Langley's concerns (1997, pp. 8–9).
   • Lack of practice time
   • Requirement of complex use of the skill
   • Organizational pattern that does not match game requirements
   • Potential to embarrass and discourage
   • No clear goals for success
   • Potential to increase management problems

They then listed six suggestions for effective student learning:

• Adequate practice time
• Requirement of less complex use of the skill
• Organizational patterns that match game requirements
• Development of student self-confidence
• Clear goals for success
• Effective management of student practice

Figure 1.10   Establish a Home for the Equipment

Use a Successful Teaching Model

How does a teacher teach a motor skill correctly? What is a correct and successful teaching model? How do teaching cues fit into this model? The following are components of a good teaching model and how cues are implemented.

- Get the students' attention! Use anticipatory sets (attention getters). This motivates the students to want to perform the skill. Make sure they pay attention to the instructions. Be enthusiastic!
- Organize the group so that everyone can see and hear. State the lesson objective by describing what is to be learned and why it is important. Your objective should be brief, simple, and direct. This should lead to a demonstration (Figure 1.11).
- Preassess your students by asking how many of them know how to perform the skill, or ask the students to perform the skill, if the skill is relatively safe.
- Demonstrate the entire skill three to five times. Show the skill from front, side, and back angles. Demonstrations should be performed as they would appear in a game situation. Move the class around so they can see the demonstration from different angles. The students should see a correct demonstration of the skill. Remember, a picture is worth a thousand words when learning a sport skill.
- After the demonstration, have the students practice the skill. This will give you time to assess their proficiency.
- Use one teaching cue at a time. This directs the students' attention to the specific area of focus.
- Have students practice the skill. You provide feedback on the cue words used in the demonstration. Use a systematic approach to giving feedback to all of your students during the class.
- Provide additional demonstrations and new cues when students have mastered previous ones.
- Review and/or demonstrate the cues during class closure. Provide the students with an opportunity to ask questions.
- Have students repeat aloud the cues for the skill. The cues will be fresh in their memories.

Figure 1.11 Demonstrate So All Can See and Hear

Integrated Activities

Integrated activities provide an opportunity to create a program that reinforces other curricular areas, such as math, reading, science, and so forth. Integrated activities help to balance the curriculum and provide a context for lifetime participation. The following are examples for your consideration:

- *Language Arts:* To reinforce writing and check for cognitive understanding, have your students write to an imaginary friend and explain how to throw a ball. To assess the affective domain, have your students write how they feel about learning sport skills, using the teaching cues, and playing the mini-games. Class discussions allow students to verbally express their experiences in using the teaching cues outside of class.
- *Fine Arts:* Draw the cues and activities. Students can draw a self-portrait of performing the overhand throw. Picture 1 depicts standing sideways. Picture 2 shows making the L with the throwing arm. Picture 3 illustrates the long step cue.
- *Theatre Arts:* Play sport charades with a partner or a small group One student acts out a sport skill, and a partner or others in a small group try to guess what the sport cue is.

Students with Disabilities

You might have the opportunity to teach children with disabilities. Be creative in developing cues and activities for these children. For example, you could put a bell around a ball for a blind student, integrate brightly colored equipment for the hearing impaired, and use balloons for the student in a wheel chair. Include all of the students. Let them participate on their own levels, see their excitement in being able to participate, and feel the emotional bonding with your students.

TOOL 7 ## AUTHENTIC ASSESSMENT: HOW DO I KNOW IT IS WORKING?

Cues Help Instructors Analyze a Skill

Some physical education teachers tend to analyze skills excessively and tell all they know (Lockhart, 1966). Cues are short and to the point, and they focus the assessment process on giving specific feedback.

Teaching cues provide students with valuable information to accompany demonstrations. Cues aid you in focusing on correct skill performance so that appropriate feedback can be given. Incorporating cues into the teaching process makes it possible for you to identify major errors quickly. For example, when students are performing the forehand stroke in tennis, and the cue is "racket head needs to finish on edge," it is easy to observe whether the racket head is on edge at the end of the stroke. It also is important to provide a reason why it is necessary to perform a particular cue accurately.

Cues Strengthen Correct Performance

A critical component of skill acquisition is that you and your students identify the parts of the skill that are being performed correctly. You can have the students work in pairs or in small groups; in this way, they can analyze their performances and give feedback to each other on one specific cue. For example, the following three cues for throwing a ball are used: (1) Take the ball straight down and graze your shorts, (2) stretch your arm way back, and (3) make an L. Student responses might include the following:

- "Hey, I liked the way you brought your arm down and grazed your shorts. That action will give you more distance."
- "Way to make an L shape with your arm! You're keeping the ball away from your head."
- "Wow! Way to stretch your arm way back! That was a great stretch. Your stretch looks just like Barry Bond's or Dale Murphy's."

This type of specific feedback increases the likelihood that the student will repeat the correct response in the near future.

Cues Help Correct Errors in Technique

"Coach, how can I go over the hurdles faster?" "How do I improve my sprint time?" "What is the best way to exchange the baton?" These are questions students might ask about track skills. Are you ready to answer these questions without criticizing or giving your student too much information?

Your challenge is to identify the cause of the problem and look for solutions. The effective use of cues avoids judgment and criticism. Cues are used to correct errors constructively. Cues help you identify the problem and provide accurate feedback to the student: for example, "Stacie, I really liked how you made a 'banana shape' when performing the long jump. This time, work on the 'jack-knife position' when you land."

Cues Help Peers Correct Errors in Technique

When students are provided with correct teaching cues, they can help give feedback to their peers. Pair students and have them observe their partner's performance. For example, if the cue given on throwing is, "Stand sideways and take a long step toward the target," a student can watch her partner and assess whether she is standing sideways and taking the long step. If her partner steps too high or takes a short step, but is standing sideways, she can provide her partner with the following feedback: "Hey, Stacie, you stood sideways. Now remember to take a longer step with your foot toward the target." This feedback emphasizes a student's correct performance, notifies her of the error, and suggests a specific way to correct the error, providing a more positive interaction.

Using Cues to Assess Students' Performance

By using cues, you have a valuable tool for assessing your students. You can assess them specifically on the cues you have taught. Your students know specific components of the skill they need to practice and how they will be assessed. This gives them an opportunity to practice the important cues. For example, a rubric can be designed with a four-point checklist. A rubric on the overhand throw might include the following:

- Stands sideways to the target
- Makes an L with the throwing arm
- Takes a long step with the leg closest to the target
- Throws hard

Decide how you want to mark the checklist. You might choose a yes-or-no format or a scale ranging from proficiency to almost there to needs more practice.

CONCLUSION

The tools outlined in this chapter help make teaching fun and exciting. Students will appreciate your expertise and retain the knowledge in a fun and caring environment. We hope this book widens your vision about teaching. We have found the cues in this book to be effective, motivating, and life altering when students are successful. To establish credibility quickly, incorporate the teaching cues in subsequent chapters to obtain the edge that is necessary to connect with your students. Have fun!

FYI

Carnegie, D. (1981). *How to win friends and influence people.* New York: Pocket Books.

Fronske, H., Abendroth-Smith, J., & Blakemore, C. (1997). The effect of critical cues on throwing efficiency of elementary school children. *The Physical Educator, 54* (2), 88–95.

Graham, G., Holt/Hale S., & Parker, M. (2000). *Children moving: A reflective approach to teaching physical education* (5th ed.) Mountain View, CA: Mayfield.

Patton, B. R., & Giffin, K. (1981). *Interpersonal communication in action: Basic text and readings* (3rd ed.) New York: Harper & Row.

Lockhart, A. (1966, May). Communicating with the learner. *Quest, VI,* 57–67.

NASPE. (1995). *Moving into the future. National standards for physical education.* St. Louis: Mosby.

Pangrazi, R. (2001). *Dynamic physical education for elementary school children.* Boston: Allyn & Bacon.

Pangrazi, R. (2001). *Dynamic physical education for elementary school children. Lesson plans.* Boston: Allyn & Bacon.

Rink, J. (1993). *Teaching physical education for learning.* St. Louis: Times Mirror/Mosby.

Woods, A., & Langley, D. (1997). Circle drills: Do they accomplish your goals? *Journal of Physical Education, Recreation, and Dance, 68*(3), 8–9.

Chapter 4

Learning the Ropes

Rope jumping develops rhythm, balance, coordination, cardiovascular endurance, and muscle strength, while providing opportunities to improve self-esteem as new skills are mastered. A rope-jumping program can be adapted to meet the needs of different ability levels or age groups, providing a challenge to each student. Promote teamwork by encouraging more proficient students to help those less able. Provide opportunities for students to work together in small groups to practice and share ideas for new skills.

Any activity can be turned into a competition—rope jumping is no exception! There are many ways to incorporate rope jumping into a curriculum that will provide opportunities for all students to excel, in one way or another.

- Skill development, rhythm, balance, coordination, endurance, and muscle strength
- Activities for the playground or to motivate learning
- Creativity to stimulate thinking skills
- Warm-up as readiness for other sports or activities
- Conditioning to enhance muscle strength, endurance, and speed

Remember to teach rope-jumping skills progressively, building on previously learned skills, and maximize opportunities for success.

SKILLS LISTED WITH CUES

This chapter presents cues for the following:

- Long rope: turning, entering jumping, and exiting
- Single-rope basic technique:
  - Double-foot jumps: side jump, front /back, straddle jump
  - Single-foot jumps: alternating steps, side step taps, heel to heel
  - Criss cross: forward cross, kicks (kick step), turn (full)
- Double Dutch: turning, entering, jumping, and exiting

EQUIPMENT TIPS

1. Long ropes (14- or 16-inch lengths) for readiness activities. Beaded (or segmented) ropes are a good choice for visibility and durability.
2. Single ropes (7-, 8-, 9-, and 10-foot lengths) for individual use. Beaded ropes turn easily with a consistent arc and are good for beginners.
3. Single-speed style (thin, vinyl cord) ropes are lighter in weight and can be turned more quickly than beaded ropes. Control and better technique are required to maintain a consistent arc. These are good for speed jumping.
4. Double Dutch ropes (14 feet is a good length for most situations). Beaded ropes are a good choice for beginners. They provide good visibility, maintain a consistent arc, and the "click" as they hit the ground is a good way for turners to monitor their rhythm. The beaded ropes can be used one at a time for long-rope activities.
5. Speed-style Double Dutch ropes are lighter in weight. They are good for fast turning, but are more difficult to control and require more experience to achieve success.
6. Cloth Double Dutch ropes are medium weight and can maintain a consistent arc. Cloth ropes can be turned at different speeds with good results and are good for stunts. These are more commonly used for competition.

TEACHING IDEAS

1. Warm up and cool down. Always include a warm-up and cool-down to reduce the chance of injury and prevent muscle soreness.
2. Long-rope readiness skills. With the youngest or least experienced jumpers, the rope need not travel over the head at first. Try some low, swinging motions to introduce the concepts of balance and timing.
3. Safety measures:
   - Proper footwear, loose and comfortable clothing
   - Adequate space for each participant
   - Clear floor area; no ropes on the floor
   - Use of proper technique
   - Avoidance of tricks requiring a sustained "squat" position, to protect knee joint

TEACHING PROGRESSION

Following the proper rope-jumping teaching progressions maximizes success every step of the way (see pages 42–50 for theose cues):

1. Long-rope readiness activities allow beginners to develop self-confidence as they improve balance and timing.
2. It is important to give everyone the opportunity to be the turner as well as the jumper.

3. Students helping each other to be successful encourages teamwork.
4. All of the elements taught in long-rope activities carry over to Double Dutch (turning, entering, jumping, and exiting).

The cues provide a progression for teaching rope-jumping skills. Start with the first sequence and follow the sequence to the end.

MINI-GAMES

A final note: There is no end to the creative possibilities that exist when rope-jumping skills are introduced. Combine rope jumping with aerobics, dance, movement activities, sport conditioning, warm-up, stations, or games. The emphasis is on improving self-esteem every step of the way. Following the progressions will ensure a successful program and successful students.

FYI

If you are interested in obtaining jump ropes or educational materials related to rope jumping, please see the following web site: www.jumprope.com

Call or write:

Heartbeat Enterprises, Inc.
6655 Dobbin Road
Columbia, MD 21045
Phone: (410) 381-8553
Fax: (410) 964-9518

LONG-ROPE READINESS SKILLS

Skill	Cue	Why?
Turning	Use a circular motion of the lower arm	To create a circular motion of the rope
	Keep a steady rhythm, listening to the "click" as the rope hits floor	To maintain constant speed of each rope as it turns
Entering	Stand close to a turner	For a quick entry
	Enter the jumping area as the rope hits the floor and moves away from the jumper	To allow the jumper as much time as possible to get in
	Jump the rope as it comes around and reaches the floor again	
Jumping	Stay centered between turners	To jump the rope where it hits the floor
	Keep jumps low to ground Match the rhythm of the turning rope	
	Note: Use a rebound jump in between jumps over the rope	To avoid "misses"
	This extra bounce or rebound will become the jump over the second rope in Double Dutch	To maintain balance
Exit	Exit the rope as it moves away from the direction of the exit	To allow the jumper as much time as possible to get out
	Exit by shoulder of a turner	To achieve a quicker exit

SINGLE-ROPE BASIC TECHNIQUE		
Skill	**Cue**	**Why?**
Start with a rope that is the correct length [Figure 4.1]	Standing with both feet on the middle of the rope, the handles should reach the armpits	The correct length of rope will encourage proper technique
Stance	Keep elbows close to the body with forearms at a 45-degree angle	
Wrist Action	Turn with the wrist after the first jump	For efficiency of motion
Jumping Action [Figure 4.2]	Relax and keep the jump as low as possible	A low jump is enough to clear the rope
Foot Action	Land on balls of feet, letting the heels touch down	To keep the Achilles' tendon stretched

Handles should reach armpits

Stand with both feet on middle of rope

Figure 4.1   Sizing a Rope

Teaching Progression

Begin with double-foot jumps—one jump per each turn of the rope. When the student achieves a steady rhythm of 90 to 100 jumps per minute, and has eliminated the "rhythm bounce," it's time to introduce the skill components:

- Double-foot jumps
- Single-foot jumps
- Criss crosses
- Kicks
- Turns

Keep elbows close to the body

Relax and keep jump as low as possible

Land on the balls of feet

Figure 4.2   Jumping Action

DOUBLE-FOOT JUMPS

Skill	Cue	Why?
Side Jump (Figure 4.3)	Legs together, mimic a "skier" action, shoulders facing forward	Skill is performed by the lower body
Front/Back	Legs together, jump forward then back	Improves balance
Straddle Jump	Alternate legs apart, legs together	Improves timing

Teaching Progression

This component includes skills that require a two-foot takeoff and landing. Variations of the basic two-foot jump include the side jump, front/back jump, straddle jump, scissors jump, cross step, twister, and wobble jump. Balancing on two feet allows the jumper to build confidence and improve timing before moving on to the next progression of single-footwork skills.

Many more possibilities exist for double-foot skills! Refer to the FYI section for information on additional teaching materials.

Shoulders facing forward

Legs together, mimic a skier's action

Figure 4.3 Side Jump

SINGLE-FOOT JUMPS		
Skill	**Cue**	**Why?**
Alternating Step	Jumper alternates feet, right to left, right, left, with each turn of the rope. Posture is erect.	To develop balance
Side Taps	Alternate feet on each jump, touching toe on the floor to the side. Jump on left foot and touch right toe to the side.	To develop timing
Heel to Heel	Alternate feet on each jump, tapping the opposite heel out to the front	To develop timing

Teaching Progression

The foundation for all single-footwork skills is alternating hops. The jumper lands first on the left foot for one turn of the rope, then on the right foot for the next turn of the rope, and so on. This skill involves a shifting of body weight from one foot to the other. A good lead-in activity is "Skipping" without the rope. When the jumper can balance on one foot at a time (static balance), the other foot is free to perform other movements (dynamic balance). The easiest skills require the jumper to balance on each foot for only one turn of the rope (i. e., side taps, heel to heel, and toe to toe). When the jumper can balance for more than one count on each foot, many more combinations are possible (e.g., heel to toe and the fling step).

There are an endless number of tricks that can be performed using alternating steps. Refer to the FYI section for more information.

CRISS CROSS

Skill	Cue	Why?
Forward Cross (Figure 4.4)	Make one regular jump over the rope	
	As the rope comes around again, cross arms in front of body, at the hips	To keep loop low enough to jump through
	Jump through the loop created by the crossed arms	To prepare for the next jump
	Arms uncross as the rope goes over the head for the next jump	

Teaching Progression

Criss cross can be taught as a double-foot jump, to allow more concentration on the arm movement. Walk through this skill to understand the dynamics. Count 1 is a regular jump. When the jumper brings the rope around for the second jump, the arms cross in front of the body, forming a loop. Check for two things: Is the loop wide enough to jump through, and is the rope touching the ground? If the answer to both questions is yes, step through the loop and bring the arms over the head to set up for the next regular jump. This time when the rope comes around to form the loop, jump through it. It may take several tries but eventually the momentum of the rope will carry it over the jumper's head and the jumper will automatically open the rope for the regular jump.

Many variations of the "cross" tricks exist. New ones are always possible. Refer to the FYI section for more information.

Cross arms in front of body at hips

Figure 4.4 Criss Cross

KICKS		
Skill	**Cue**	**Why?**
Kick Step (Figure 4.5)	Hop on left foot on the first turn of the rope while lifting the right foot Hop over the rope with the left foot again while kicking the right foot out in front	To set up for the kick

Teaching Progression

Begin this component with the hops drill. While turning the rope, students begin with one single jump on the left foot, then one single jump on the right foot. Continue with two jumps on the left, two jumps on the right, up to five jumps on each foot. Playing music with an appropriate beat will help the jumpers maintain their rhythm. All the skills in the kicks component involve alternating two hops on each foot. The first hop is the lift, and the second is the kick to the front or to the side. If a jumper has difficulty with the kick, more practice may be needed on the alternating hops drill. For further variations on the "kick" component, refer to the FYI section.

Hop over rope with left foot

Kick the right foot out in front

Figure 4.5   Kick Step

TURNS		
Skill	**Cue**	**Why?**
Full Turn	Make one regular jump facing forward	
	Make a quarter turn to the left while "swishing" the rope on the left side of the body	To set up for the "backward jump" (turning the rope over the head from front to back, and jumping over it)
	Make another quarter turn to the left while taking a backward jump. The rope is now in front of the body.	
	"Carry" the rope the final 180 degrees while turning around to face front again and pull the rope under the feet	

Teaching Progression

A variation of the full turn involves making the 360-degree rotation in one count! Try this without the rope first. Jump and spin in the air, landing on the same spot and facing the same direction. If the jumper is successful without a rope, try it with a rope, using the "carry" technique, adding two bounces before the spin for a smoother take-off.

Skill components wrap-up: It is important to follow the progressions when teaching new skills. Having a strong foundation in the basic skills makes it more fun and rewarding. Create new steps and combinations. Practice the footwork patterns until they are mastered. Then add arm crosses or side swishes for new tricks. Practice with music for fun and timing practice.

DOUBLE DUTCH

Skill	Cue	Why?
Turning	Using the circular turning motion, turn ropes toward the center, with the rope hitting the floor alternately	To create the circular motion of the ropes
	Focus on the center spot	This is where the jumper will be
	Establish a steady rhythm	To help the jumper establish a rhythm
Entering	Stand next to turner, watching the closest rope	For a quick entry
	Enter as the near rope passes the jumper's face. The near rope will be the one that comes around to be jumped first.	This is where the ropes are the most "open" for entry
Jumping	Keep jumping! The second rope is coming around. Keep jump low and relaxed, but get off the ground.	A high jump is not necessary to clear the rope
Exiting	Jump one last time over the first rope jumped. Exit on the opposite side, in a diagonal line from the entry.	Exiting on the diagonal is the quickest way out
Helpful Hints	Ask the jumper to look for the "open mouth" when the ropes are in position for the entry and exit	Remember the three L's *look* (for the rope to pass the jumper's face), *listen* (to the beat of the ropes), and *leap!*
	Try to visualize the entry into the ropes (the open mouth), and the exit, with concentration on the closest rope	

Teaching Progression

Double Dutch combines all the elements of long rope and single rope into an exciting and challenging activity. To achieve success, the emphasis should be on teamwork. Review the section on long rope and its four basic skills—turning, entering, jumping, and exiting.

Double Dutch wrap-up: Jumpers of all ability levels can participate in Double Dutch following the progressions outlined. Teamwork is an essential component for success. Pair up stronger turners with weaker ones for practice turning. Encourage students to create new tricks and teach them to others. Work toward partner activities, routines, turner involvement, and props (a basketball, for instance) in the ropes.

Chapter 5

Advanced Cues for Locomotor Skills

Teaching students good posture and the advanced locomotor skills helps them learn the basic foundations for many sport skills. Learning to jump or hop correctly helps them later with a spike in volleyball or lay-up in basketball. Performing these skills gives students a great fitness workout. The cues in this chapter are designed by track specialists. The skills presented are performed by track athletes as part of their daily drills. Teach these advanced locomotor skills and provide your students with a jump start for learning the foundation of movement.

SKILLS LISTED WITH CUES

This chapter presents cues for the following skill: posture, as it relates to standing, walking, and walking activities. The locomotor skills include walking, jogging, vertical and horizontal jumps, hopping, skipping, galloping, leaping, and sliding.

EQUIPMENT TIPS

1. The students should have a good pair of tennis shoes.
2. You should provide upbeat music and a CD player.

TEACHING IDEA

Pair the students and let them give feedback to each other on each locomotor skill.

TEACHING PROGRESSIONS

1. Warm up the students with jogging and dynamic stretches (see Chapter 7).
2. Teach the skills in order: standing, walking, jogging, skipping, galloping, vertical and horizontal jumps, sliding, and leaping.

MINI-GAMES

Play upbeat music, and when the music changes, have the children practice another locomotor skill. The music adds fun and rhythm to these skills.

FYI

Suggested Reading:

Danforth, W. H. (1991). *I dare you*. St. Louis: American Youth Foundation.

I Dare You Committee
American Youth Foundation
1315 Ann Avenue
St. Louis, MO 63104-9902
Phone: (314) 772-2889

POSTURE		
Skill	**Cue**	**Why?**
Standing (Figure 5.1)		
Chin	Pull in the chin	
Chest	Chest is up	Keeps shoulders back
Abdomen	Pull abdomen in	Pulls hips under shoulders
Back	Back is flat	Enhances body posture awareness
Test (Figure 5.2)	Stand up straight to the wall, toes touching. If posture is correct, the wall will just touch your chest, and no other part of your body. Your nose will miss the wall about an inch.	
Walking (Figure 5.3)		
Feet	Heel, toe push-off	More power
Arms	Drive the elbows back, arms at 90 degrees, thumbs on forefingers	More efficient, better workout Helps prevent hands from going numb
Chin	Pull yourself to attention	Creates a "pillar"
Chest	Chin in	
	Chest up	
Abdomen	Abdomen in	

WALKING ACTIVITIES

1. Walk as if you were walking past a general.
2. Push out your third vest button.
3. Take a walk before school, during lunch, or after school. Work on good posture. After a while, the students will get into the habit of walking tall.

Back
is flat

Pull in
the chin

Pull abdomen
in, chest up

Figure 5.1   Standing

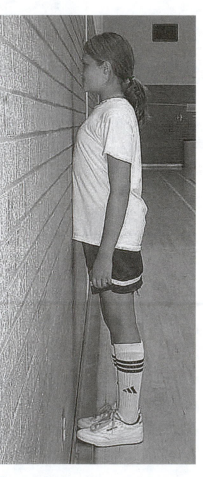

Wall just
touches chest

Nose misses
wall by an inch

Toes touch
wall

Figure 5.2   Standing Test

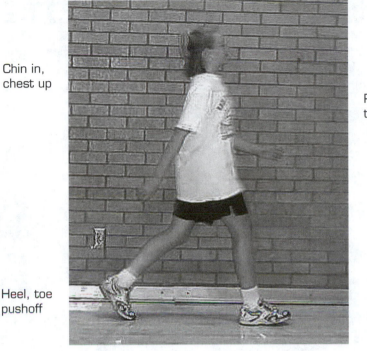

Chin in, chest up

Pull yourself to attention

Heel, toe pushoff

Figure 5.3   Walking

RUNNING		
Skill	**Cue**	**Why?**
Finger Action	Thumb rests on forefinger (like holding a pencil)	Maintains a loose forearm and shoulder
Foot Action	Run on lower ball of foot. Transfer weight to heel (almost flatfooted). Like "pawing" the ground	Foot contact needs to be under the hip. This is more efficient. A heel strike breaks momentum of stride, whereas lower ball of foot gives better push-off (not on your toes).
Elbow Action	Elbows in, brush hips	
Face/Neck	RELAX face, neck, shoulders and arms (lips and cheeks jiggle like Jell-O)	Easier breathing decreases energy expenditure
Posture	Run tall, as if you have a book on your head	Good posture builds self-confidence and better social skills

VERTICAL—HORIZONTAL JUMPS

Skill	Cue	Why?
Vertical Jump (Figure 5.4)		
Stance	Feet shoulder width apart	Good base of support
Leg Action	Bend knees, like sitting in a chair	Maximum angle of push-off
Arm Action	Swing arms backward to shoulder level	
Execution Action	Push off with balls of feet	
	Swing arms forward and up, jump and try to touch the sky.	Creates vertical momentum
Horizontal Jump		
Arm Action	Same cues as for vertical jump, except swing arms forward and up	
Leg Action	Jump forward	Creates horizontal and vertical momentum

Swing arms backward to shoulder level

Bend knees like sitting in a chair

Figure 5.4 Vertical Jump

HOPPING

Skill	Cue	Why?
Foot off Ground	Lift knee parallel to make an L shape while hopping	Increase distance and power
Foot on Ground	Push off ball of foot and hop	Maintain spring, transfer force up instead of into ground
Arm Action	Circle arm motion like chicken wings—elbows out, thumbs in by armpits	

SKIPPING

Skill	Cue	Why?
Right Leg	Bring knee up like you are running in L shape	Increases stride length and vertical height
Left Elbow	Opposite elbow drives back, thumb in pocket	Creates a 90 degree angle with arms which is more energy efficient. Keeps momentum moving in a positive direction.
Right Elbow	Elbow forward and up to make an L	
Left Leg	Push off the ball of foot, hop and land on the same foot	Shortens contact with ground
Motion of Skipping	Take a step and hop, step and hop. "Step, hop, step, hop"	Minimizes breaking action which will slow you down

GALLOPING

Skill	Cue	Why?
Foot Action	One foot ahead of other foot	
Leading Leg	Keep same foot ahead and travel	
Foot Action	Contact ball of foot	Contact with ground is under hip, acting as a pulling action instead of pushing
Arm Action	Hold arms as if holding reins while riding a horse	
	Rocking motion, like riding a stick horse	

LEAPING

Skill	Cue	Why?
Leg Action	Push off one foot Land on other foot	
Landing Action	Land quietly	Indication of an active landing Foot is contacting ground under hip
Arm Action	Swing arms high and straight in opposition with legs (90 degrees front 120 degrees back)	
Chest and Head Action	Lift with chest and head	

SLIDING

Skill	Cue	Why?
Stance	Wide stance Sit in your stance like a bull rider Bend knees	Lowers center of gravity. Increases stability.
Leg Action	Slide lead foot out and push off ball of trail leg and transfer weight on to lead leg.	
	Return trail leg to Beg stance.	
	Maintain feet 6 inches apart on slide	Lowers center of gravity. Increases stability.

Chapter 6

Dynamic Stretching and Pillar Exercises

Before beginning any type of physical activity, an adequate warm-up and stretching routine is imperative. A pre-activity warm-up increases blood flow to muscles, decreases the chance of injury, and decreases post-exercise soreness and discomfort. Students should warm up for a minimum of 20 to 60 minutes, depending on the activity to be performed and the duration of the activity. Highly explosive exercises, such as sprinting, jumping, and activities requiring quick changes of direction, require longer warm-ups. Recreational jogging and cycling require a shorter warm-up. In this chapter, we introduce a new and improved way of warming up called *dynamic stretching*.

Dynamic stretching combines stretching and traditional warm-up activities in one activity. This form of warm-up increases muscular flexibility and motor-muscular coordination, and enhances the neuromuscular system by reviving the muscular body instead of depressing it. Dynamic stretching differs from the traditional static stretching routine because all stretching activities are performed as a continuous motion or movement. (Static stretching involves stationary movement.)

SKILLS LISTED WITH CUES

This chapter presents cues for the following:

- Becoming a pillar
- Dynamic stretches
- Pillar cues
- Pillar exercises

EQUIPMENT TIPS

1. Play music during the activity.
2. Wear a good pair of tennis shoes.
3. Wear clothing that allows free movement.

TEACHING IDEAS

1. Before beginning the routine, you must be reminded that the body should act as a "solid pillar" (see Chapter 7). The head should align on top of the shoulders, the shoulders over the hips, and the hips over the feet. The most important area of the pillar is the center, or "core."
2. The core consists of the area between the middle of the thighs to the bottom of the rib cage, both front and back.
3. Pillar exercises have been developed to strictly target the core. When performing any activity, the first area to falter and hinder performance is the core. If students recognize this and perform exercises to enhance their pillar, especially the core, they will be increasing their performance and athletic longevity.

TEACHING PROGRESSIONS

1. Jogging at least three laps around the gym, or jogging 5 minutes to warm up the muscles
2. Dynamic exercises
3. Sprinting drills
4. Core exercises
5. Game
6. Static stretches

MINI-GAMES

1. Jogging could be an introductory activity for the warm-up and dynamic stretches. Sprinting drills and core exercises could be the fitness and skill activity. End the class with a fun game that works on sprinting skills—for example, tag games or a major sport, such as basketball or soccer.
2. See Chapter 7 for game ideas for sprinting.
3. Ultimate Frisbee is a fun game with which to end a class.
4. Tag Games
5. Soccer
6. Quad Ball
7. Basketball

FYI

Jamie Hall/Bennion
USA Track and Field Level 2 Coach
Mountain Crest Head Track and Field Coach, Hyrum, UT
Rocky Mountain Elite Track and Field Coach, Logan, UT
Phone: (801) 756-4689
Email: jamiebennion@hotmail.com

BECOMING A PILLAR/BODY AWARENESS

Skill	Cue	Why?
Become a "Pillar"	Head over shoulders, shoulders over hips, hips over feet whether in a vertical or horizontal position	To become aware of body alignment
Body Awareness	Know where and what your body is doing	
Gradual to Aggressive	Perform activities in a gradual to aggressive fashion	To avoid injury and for sequential warm-up
Focus on the "Core"	Perform pillar exercises	To develop a strong core, enhance performance, and increase athletic longevity
Complete Body Coverage	Start the progression with the head and work your way down to the feet	For complete body warm-up and coverage

Teaching Progression

Each exercise, unless otherwise noted, should be performed in the following manner: exercise, jog 10 meters, exercise, jog 10 meters. Continue the activity for a total of 40 meters.

DYNAMIC STRETCHES

Skill	Cue	Why?
Neck Rolls	Roll neck in a clockwise, then counterclockwise direction three times	Relieve tension in neck and shoulders
Windmill (Forward)	Big arm circles in a forward, opposing windmill action	Loosen shoulders
Windmill (Backward)	Big arm circles in a backward, opposing windmill action	Loosen shoulders
Hip Circles	Rotating only at the hip. Circle in clockwise, then counterclockwise direction three times	Loosen hips
Walking Lunges (Figure 6.1)	Touch hand on the ground, lunge with opposite leg four times, then jog 10 meters Keep head and back straight	Increase strength and flexibility in quads and hamstring muscles
High Kicks	Kick foot high to head, four times each foot; jog 10 meters	Increase flexibility of hamstrings and lower back muscles
Calf Stretch	Stretch each calf for six counts, then jog 10 meters	Increase flexibility of calf muscles; prevent injury
Ankle Rolls	Roll each ankle clockwise, then counterclockwise three times each ankle	Loosen up ankle joints

Head over shoulders

Back straight

Lunge

Figure 6.1 Walking Lunges

After the dynamic stretches, the following sprinting drills should be performed next. Perform these drills in the order listed.

SPRINTING DRILLS		
Skill	**Cue**	**Why?**
Pawing Action	See Chapter 7	These drills increase blood flow to muscles
Walking A's	See Chapter 7	
Skipping A's	See Chapter 7	
Running A's	See Chapter 7	

Next, work on making a good pillar.

A GOOD PILLAR		
Skill	**Cue**	**Why?**
Pillar	Head over shoulders, shoulders over hips, hips over feet	For body awareness and alignment
Tight Stomach	Stomach muscles should be tight, pulling the hips under the rib cage	This is proper posture
Gradual to Aggressive	Perform exercises from gradual to more aggressive	To avoid injury

Then you can work on these pillar exercises.

PILLAR EXERCISES

Skill	Cue	Why?
Iron Cross (Face Up)	Lie on ground (face up) with arms straight out to side. Swing leg across body to opposite hand.	To stretch lower back muscles and hamstrings
Iron Cross (Face Down)	Lie on ground (face down) with arms straight out to side. Swing leg across body to opposite hand.	To stretch lower back muscles, quadriceps, stomach muscles, and chest
Bicycle	Lie on ground, hips propped up under hands, spin the legs in a bicycle motion, forward and backward	Work on balance, hamstring strength, flexibility, and strength
Scissors Kick	Hands under hips, touch toes on the ground behind the head in a swinging, scissors motion	Balance, hamstring strength, and flexibility
Cat Stretches	On all fours, stretch leg back and up	Increase strength in hamstrings and lower back
Fire Hydrants	On all fours, keeping knee bent, lift leg to the side (like a dog at a fire hydrant)	Increase strength and flexibility of hip flexors
Hip Circles	On all fours, bring one knee to chest, circle knee out to side, extend back. Repeat.	Increase strength and flexibility of hip flexors
Standing Leg Swings	Facing a wall, swing leg in a frontal and sagittal plane	Increases flexibility of lower back, hamstrings, and quadriceps
All-Americans	Hold push-up position for time	Increases strength of pillar and core. Body alignment awareness.
Front (Figure 6.2)	Head over shoulders, shoulder over hips, hips over feet	
Side (Figure 6.3)	Body is sideways Support body on one hand Tight stomach Pull buttocks in	Same as above

PILLAR EXERCISES

Skill	Cue	Why?
Back (Figure 6.4)	Push hips up Shoulders, hips, and feet in line with body Arms straight	
Advanced All-Americans	Hold push-up position on hands and then drop to elbows or lift one foot or hand off the ground	
Bananas	Lie on back and, for time, lift shoulder and feet off of the ground 6 inches	Increases stomach and quadriceps muscle strength
Hang-Glider (Figure 6.5)	Lie on stomach and, for time, lift the chest and legs off of the ground as high as possible	Increases back muscle strength

Teaching Progression

Pillar exercises can be performed prior to and after a workout. Remember to watch alignment!

Shoulders over hips, hips over feet

Head over shoulders

Hold push-up position

Figure 6.2   All-Americans (Front)

Pull buttocks

Tight stomach

Focus on making a pillar

Figure 6.3   All-Americans (Side)

Shoulders, hips,
and feet in line

Push
hips up

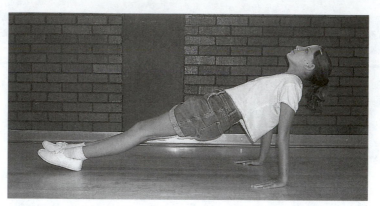

Arms straight

Figure 6.4   All-Americans (Back)

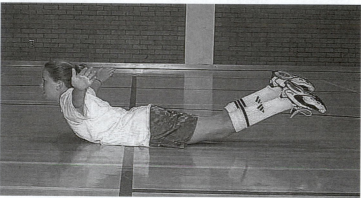

Lift chest and
legs off ground
as high as
possible

Figure 6.5   Hang-Glider

Chapter 7

Sprinting Drills

F ew sports are performed without the component of sprinting. Whether playing soccer, basketball, tennis, or track, sprinting is a key factor of the sport. Research has shown that efficient and effective sprinting is a result of sound leg action (Coker, 1998; Winkler et al., 1986). To be more specific, sprinting is characterized by greater knee flexion upon recovery of the free leg from back to front. Having the heel pulled close to the buttocks and the knee parallel to the ground accomplishes this greater knee flexion. If the heel is not pulled tight to the buttocks, a long lever results. A basic tenet of physics is that a longer lever will move through a plane slower than will a short lever. When the leg is properly bent and the heel is pulled to the buttocks, the limb will move through the cycling action much quicker, putting the leg in an optimal position for the next stride. With the increase of efficiency in one's running pattern comes an increased stride frequency and stride length, which is directly influenced by proper technique (Winkler et al., 1986).

For these drills to be performed correctly and efficiently, it is important to note and explain the "pillar" concept as it relates to sprinting. Pretend that your body forms a pillar from head to toe. This would mean that your head is over your shoulders, your shoulders are over your hips, and your hips are over your feet. Posture is very important in every activity that involves running. It is the foundation of proper form and helps prevent injury. Before teaching any of the sprint drills, emphasize the pillar concept.

Specific drills can assist you in teaching elementary and middle school students how to sprint properly and efficiently. These drills benefit students by developing motor control, strength, and muscular endurance. Students will be successful in their running and an increase in speed will be the direct result (Coker, 1998).

Although some students have an innate ability to sprint fast and others will struggle, all can be taught to sprint faster. Teaching proper technique prevents bad habits from forming and increases body awareness and self-esteem. When students experience increased speed, their confidence rises, setting the stage for participating in a variety of sports and activities.

Even college athletes, from football players to softball players, benefit from learning the basics of sprint mechanics that they missed during their childhood. Imagine the jump start a student could have by learning these basic drills early. When the mechanics of sprinting are learned early, you can spend more time developing and refining many other sport skills.

SKILLS LISTED WITH CUES

This chapter presents cues for the following: pillar, sprinting (pawing action, walking A's, skipping A's, and running A's), sprint acceleration, transition, and full speed.

EQUIPMENT TIPS

1. Upbeat music and a CD player
2. A good pair of running shoes

TEACHING IDEAS

1. All drills should be performed on the lower balls of the feet. No heel contact with the ground should occur.
2. Teaching proper technique prevents students from forming bad habits and increases body awareness and self-esteem.
3. Be sensitive to developmental characteristics. Some children may have physical limitations.
4. Establish a warm, supportive climate, in which students are not making fun of each other.
5. Safety considerations
   - Make sure that students are adequately warmed up before practicing the sprinting drills. When they practice the drills, look to see if they are overexerting themselves. Be aware of progressions and where your students' abilities range. Remember: Not too fast, not too much, not too soon. Be aware of fatigue, and give the students the option to rest during the sprinting drills. One of the signs of fatigue is a child who does not want to practice the next drill.
   - Running surfaces need to be safe, free of holes and uneven ground. Adequate space needs to be provided for the students to practice the drills. Be aware of environmental considerations such as heat, water availability, appropriate clothing, and athletic shoes.

TEACHING PROGRESSIONS

1. These drills are presented in a progression from simple to complex. Once the drills have been taught and understood, it is not necessary to perform them in an exact order. It is up to you to provide variety and whether to focus on one component more than another. All drills should be performed on the lower balls of the feet. No heel contact should occur with the ground. This allows for optimal contact on the ground directly under the hip.

2. It is recommended that elementary students begin with a minimum of three sets of 30 meters for all four drills and a maximum of eight sets (Table 7.1). Before having students participate in these drills, they should do an appropriate warm-up to stimulate blood flow to the deeper muscle tissues.

MINI-GAMES

1. See Chapter 6 for game ideas on sprinting.
2. The warm-up could be used as an introductory activity, lasting 2 to 3 minutes. The dynamic stretching, sprinting drills, core exercises, and building striders could be used for an 8- to 10-minute fitness activity in a track and field unit. These should be done every day during the unit.
3. These warm-ups and drills could be included in sports that require sprinting, such as basketball, football, soccer, Ultimate Frisbee, and softball.
4. Segments of these warm-ups and drills should be included in your curriculum every day. Practice two of the drills for 5 minutes. The keys are repetition and emphasizing the cues and correcting errors.

TABLE 7.1 DRILL SCHEDULE

Day/Week	Running Drills 1–4
Days 1–2	3–8 sets of 30 m each drill
Days 3–5	5 sets of 20 m each drill (to allow for soreness)
Week 2	7 sets of 30 m each drill
Week 3	8 sets of 30 m each drill
Week 4	7 sets of 30 m each drill
Week 5	6 sets of 30 m each drill
Week 6	5 sets of 30 m each drill
Week 7	5 sets of 20 m each drill
Week 8	4 sets of 20 m each drill
Week 9	4 sets of 20 m each drill

FYI

Coker, C. (1998, January/February). Performance excellence: Making the most of natural speed. *Strategies, 11*(3), 10–12.

Pfaff, D., Myers, B., Light, R., Freeman, W., & Winkler, G. (1991). *USA Track & Field Level II. Coaching education program: The jumps.* Indianpolis, IN: The Athletic Congress, TAC, USA.

Sefeik, G., Schexnayder, I., Deem, A., & Freeman, W. (1996, July). *Sprints, hurdles, relays. Revised.* Indianpolis, IN: USATF Coaching Education Program Level II Course.

Winkler, G., Seagrave, L., Gambetta, V., et al. (1986). *Sprints and hurdles. Coaching Certification Level II.* Indianpolis, IN: The Athletic Congress, TAC, USA.

Winkler, G., & Schexnayder, I. (1998, July). *Level three coaching seminar.* Baton Rouge, LA: United States of America Track & Field.

PILLAR

Skill	Cue	Why?
Pillar Cues (Figure 7.1A)	Critical for many sport skills	Foundation of correct body posture in most sport skills
Head Position	Head over shoulders	Creates more efficiency in their sprinting technique
Shoulder Position	Shoulders over hips	
Hip Position	Hips over feet	
	Make a pillar with your torso when performing sprinting drills and sprinting	

See Chapter 6 for additional dynamic stretching and pillar exercises.

Head over shoulders
Shoulders over hips
Hips over feet

Make a pillar
with your torso

Figure 7.1A   Pillar

SPRINTING DRILLS

Skill	Cue	Why?
Toe Action	Toe up	To allow foot contact. To be as close under the hips as possible. This allows sprinting to be a pushing action, instead of a pulling action. Decreases time spent on the ground and places the foot in an optimal position to come up under the hip, and eliminates "dangle time" (leg extended behind you after it leaves the ground).
Heel Action	Heel up	To shorten the lever as quickly as possible by bringing the heel directly under the buttocks. Avoids "dangle time."
Knee Action	Knee up Make a backwards L Thigh parallel	Increases stride length
Arm Action	Hold arms at 90-degree angle. Fingers come to the eye on the front side. Don't pass the hip on the back side. Fingers "eye to hip"	
Pillar	Run tall and make a pillar with torso Head over shoulders Shoulders over hips Hips over feet	

FOUR PROGRESSIVE SPRINT DRILLS

Drill 1: Pawing Action

In this drill, students focus on pulling the heel directly under the buttocks and raising the thigh to a position parallel to the ground. The drill is performed by standing sideways, placing one hand on a wall, and raising the opposite leg so the thigh is parallel to the ground. The ready position is knee parallel to the ground, heel under the buttocks, and toes flexed toward the knee. The student then makes a pawing action on the ground, similar to that of a bull threatening to charge. Through out the whole sequence, the toe stays flexed, emphasizing contact on the ground directly under the hip.

Drill 2: Walking A's

Walking A's (see Figure 7.1B) are very similar to the pawing action. Begin by standing in the start position (knee parallel to ground, toe flexed, and heel to buttocks). Perform the pawing action one leg after the other and begin moving forward. Emphasize the cues of toe up, knee up, and heel up.

Drill 3: Skipping A's

This drill (Figure 7.2) emphasizes the powerful snap of the leg to the ground under the hip. A skip is performed. The student focuses on the cues—thigh parallel, toe up, and heel up—in addition to placing the foot in the optimal position under the hip upon contact with the ground.

Drill 4: Running A's

This drill is sometimes known as "High Knees." Running A's put all the drills together and emphasize frequency of contacts with the ground, not distance traveled.

Knee parallel to ground

Toe up

Heel up

Figure 7.1B   Walking A's

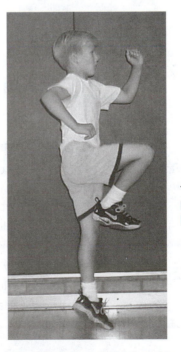

Perform a skip

Ball of foot lands under hip

Toe up, knee up, heel up

Figure 7.2   Skipping A's

SPRINT ACCELERATION

A sprint acceleration is a gradual acceleration from a standing position to full speed over 100 meters. The purpose is to develop and rehearse the conceptual model of acceleration and transitioning to full speed.

SPRINT ACCELERATION		
Skill	**Cue**	**Why?**
Acceleration (Initial 15–30 meters)	Push, push, push on the balls of feet	More time needs to be spent on the ground during the initial acceleration phase, to obtain a faster top-end speed
	Low heel recovery (heels don't come above the opposite knees)	
	Toe up	
Transition (Through 50 meters)	Uniformly progress from an emphasis on pushing to a "pawing action"	Allows sprinter to maintain speed that has been generated from the acceleration phase
	Toe up, heel up, knee up	When the knees drop, deceleration occurs. The longer a sprinter can keep the knees up, the longer she will maintain full speed.
	Body must be a "pillar"	
	Transition from low heel recovery to high heel recovery (heel under buttocks)	
Full Speed (Figure 7.3)	Toe up, heel up, knee up	When the knees drop, deceleration occurs. The longer a sprinter can keep the knees up, the longer he will maintain full speed.
	Maintain knee parallel to ground	
	Hold arms at 90-degree angle	
	Fingers "eye to hip"	
	Make a pillar with your torso	
	Run tall	
	Ball of foot lands under hip	

Arms at 90°
angle, fingers
eye to hip

Run tall

Make a pillar
with your torso

Figure 7.3　Sprinting

Chapter 8

Throwing, Catching, Striking, and Kicking

Every student should have the opportunity to be taught how to throw, catch, strike, and kick. Students who experience success in these four sport skills could catch the spark of confidence to participate in a variety of sport activities for the rest of their lives.

SKILLS LISTED WITH CUES

The skills presented in this chapter include throwing right- and left-handed, catching, catching above and below the waist, throwing a football, catching a football, serving underhanded, serving overhanded, punting a ball, and catching a punted ball.

EQUIPMENT TIPS

1. Five to 10 tennis balls for each student when practicing outside
2. One soft softball for each student when throwing inside against a wall
3. One 8-inch web or regular Nerf ball for each student, or leather volleyballs
4. One web or Nerf football for two students
5. Twelve round polyspots
6. Distance markers: orange cones with an attached sign indicating yardage, such as 10, 20, 30, 40 yards, and so on
7. Thirty brightly colored vests

TEACHING IDEAS

Fronske, Abendroth-Smith, and Blakemore (1997) found that students who didn't know how to throw also didn't know how to catch. Have your students practice throwing first. The following guidelines are suggested when teaching throwing:

- Provide each student with five to 10 tennis balls. (Tennis balls seem to fit the students' hands.) Old tennis balls are inexpensive and can be found at most universities, high school physical education departments, or sports clubs that offer tennis as part of their program. Big, plastic soap containers can be used to carry the balls.
- Place the tennis balls on a long field (five to 10 balls at each spot) about 2 feet apart. If inside, provide each student with one soft softball to throw against a wall.
- Be sure to have your students practice with their right and left hands.

SKILL PROGRESSION DRILLS

1. Have students throw to a wall or outside in the field.
2. Throwing is taught first, then catching. When these two skills are mastered, the students are ready to play Speed Throw and Throwbee.
3. Next, teach punting and catching with an 8-inch ball. Play Throwbee with a kick.
4. Next, teach throwing, catching, and kicking and catching a punt using a football. Play Philadelphia Football.

MINI-GAMES

The following games are designed to help students practice the specific skills of throwing, catching, kicking (punting), and striking in a game situation. Every student has the opportunity to respond to many touches of the ball, to play each position, and to be successful. Your students will have fun practicing new skills in a great game. Emphasize the cues during these mini-games.

1. *Speed Throw:* Play Speed Throw after the students have demonstrated their ability to throw the ball around the bases with good throwing form. Speed Throw is a game played with an 8-inch Nerf soccer ball and six players (pitcher; catcher; first, second, and third base; and a batter at home plate). The object of the game is for the batter to run the bases before the ball is thrown home. The pitcher throws the ball to the batter; the batter then throws the ball back to the pitcher. The batter now runs around the bases and back to home. The pitcher throws to first, first throws back to the pitcher. Pitcher throws to second, second throws back to the pitcher. Pitcher throws

to third, third throws back to the pitcher. Pitcher throws home to the catcher, before the runner reaches home. A point is scored by the batting team when the runner gets home before the ball reaches home. Everyone then rotates a position. The batter now goes to third base, third to second, second to first, to pitcher, and pitcher to catcher, and the catcher then becomes the batter.

Variation: Challenge the players to use a soft softball; throw with left hand.

2. *Throwbee:* Throwbee is played on a grass field and is like Ultimate Frisbee. Instead of a disc, an 8-inch ball is used to play the game. A team consists of four to eight players. Rules for the game include the following:
   - Start the game with a thrown ball to the opposing team.
   - The ball should be caught in the air or after one bounce. The player catching the ball has the option to run three steps with the ball or to throw it to a teammate.
   - If the thrown ball is missed, the other team takes possession where the player missed the catch.
   - One point is scored when a player catches the ball across her team's endline.

3. *Philadelphia Football:* Philadelphia Football is played like Ultimate Frisbee on a grass field. Instead of a disc, a football is used to play the game. There are four to eight players on a team. Rules for the game include the following:
   - To start the game, the ball is kicked (punted) to the opposing team.
   - The ball should be caught in the air or after one bounce. The player catching the ball must throw the ball to a teammate.
   - If the ball is dropped, the defensive team takes possession where the player missed the catch.
   - One point is scored when a player catches the ball across his team's endline. Teams switch ends of the field after each point.
   - A player is permitted three steps, if catching the ball on the run.
   - A defender cannot steal the ball or knock the ball from the player who is throwing the ball.
   - Each player on the team should have the opportunity to kick (punt) after a point is scored.

4. *Mini-Volleyball Tennis:* This game gives students practice striking and catching the ball in a game situation. The students are encouraged to move quickly on the court to "beat" the ball to the spot. This is a great lead-up game for volleyball. Rules for the game include the following:
   - Set up different types of nets, such as those for volleyball, Pickle-Ball, or tennis.
   - Have 3-on-3 or 4-on-4 games. Each team plays on one side of the court.
   - The game is started by a player standing close (students choose where) to the net. A player should serve the ball over the net, using an underhand or overhand serve. Servers decide when they are ready to move farther back.
   - A point is scored by the server when the ball goes over the net and lands within the court boundaries. Service continues until a service is caught by a member of the other team. Rotate players into the serve position after each side-out.

- A point is scored by the opposing team if they catch the served ball. Side-out now occurs.
- Play the game to 15 points. A team must win by 2 points.
- Call the ball when attempting to catch the ball.
- Communicate like volleyball players.

FYI

Research Article

Fronske, H., Abendroth- Smith, J., & Blakemore, C. (1997). The effect of critical cues on throwing efficiency of elementary school children. *The Physical Educator, 54*(2), 88–95.

Equipment

Web balls can be ordered from the following company:

Sportime
One Sport Way
Atlanta, GA 30340
www.sportime.com

Phone orders: (800) 283-5700
Fax orders: (800) 845-1535

THROWING—RIGHT- AND LEFT-HANDED

Skill	Cue	Why?
Right-Handed		
Stance	Stand sideways	More power; ball will go farther
Leg Action	Take a long step toward the target	More power; ball will go farther
Arm Action	Stretch the arm down, brush the shorts	
Elbow Action (Figure 8.1)	Stretch the arm way back and make an L	More power
Release Point (Figure 8.2)	Release at 2:00 position	Ball does not go too low or too high
Follow-Through	Turn palm out on follow-through	More speed on the ball
Left-Handed	Same as above	
Release Point	Release at 10:00 position	

Skill Progressions

1. *Always* start throwing the ball against a wall or in an open field. In an open field, throw 10 tennis balls per student. Have them throw and retrieve the balls. This works on fitness at the same time.
2. Use small balls to start. Why? Small balls will fit the size of the students' hands.
3. Throw with both right and left hands.
4. Progress to an 8-inch playground ball.
5. Tennis balls and soft softballs are good ones to throw.
6. Pair students. Students can observe each other and give feedback on the cue given.

Mini-Game: Speed Throw

Stretch the arm way back and make an "L"

Stand sideways to target

Take a long step

Figure 8.1 Throwing Elbow Action

Release at 2:00

Turn palm out on follow through

Figure 8.2 Throwing Release Point

CATCHING		
Skill	**Cue**	**Why?**
Catching Basics (Figure 8.3)		
Hand Position	Spread fingers—Big hands	More surface area on the ball
Arm Action	Reach out and pull ball in	The ball won't hit the student
Finger Action	Squeeze ball like clay	More chance of holding onto the ball
	Quiet, soft hands when you catch ball	More absorption of the ball
Eyes	Keep watching ball all the way into body	Students have a tendency to look away
Catching above Waist		
Hand Position (Figure 8.4)	Thumbs up Wide fingers	Most effective surface area for hands. Hands are big and in best position to catch the ball.
Catching below Waist		
Hand Position (Figure 8.5)	Pinkies down Wide fingers	Most effective surface area for hands. Hands are big and in best position to catch the ball.

Skill Progressions

1. Use 8-inch balls first. Teach throwing first. Progress to throwing and catching with a partner.
2. Progress to smaller balls, like soft softballs and tennis balls.
3. Catch high balls and low balls. Catch short balls and long balls.
4. See how fast your students can get rid of the ball and catch the ball. The first to catch 15 to 25 in a row wins.

Mini-Games: Speed Throw and Throwbee without the kick

Watch the
ball all way
into body

Reach out and
pull ball in

Big hands,
quiet hands,
soft hands

Figure 8.3   Catching a Chest-High Ball

Reach out

Thumbs up

Wide fingers

Figure 8.4   Catching a High Ball

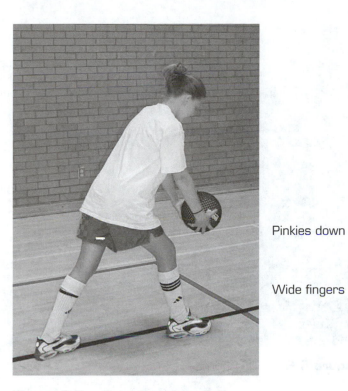

Pinkies down

Wide fingers

Figure 8.5   Catching a Low Ball

THROWING A FOOTBALL		
Skill	**Cue**	**Why?**
Grip (Figure 8.6)	Grab top of ball like holding a soda pop can or a fish's head	More surface area on ball; better control
	Fingerpad hold, laces	Better grip
	Spread fingers	
Stance and Leg Action	Stand sideways	To get rid of the football fast
	Short to medium step	
Throwing Action (Figure 8.7)	Stretch arm way back; make an L shape	Ball does not get batted away
Release Point	Release at 2:00 position (left-handed release at 10:00). Football points upward.	Ball will go at correct angle
Follow-Through	Turn palm out	More power on the football

Finger
pads hold
laces

Grab top of ball
like holding a
soda pop can

Spread fingers

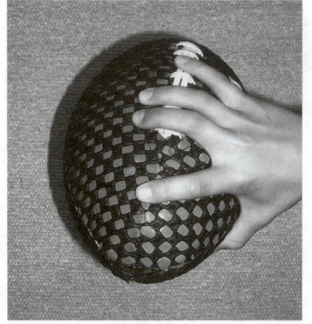

Figure 8.6   Grip Football

Stand
sideways

Stretch the arm
way back

Make an "L"
shape

Short to
medium
step

Figure 8.7   Thowing a Football Left-Handed

CATCHING A FOOTBALL

Skill	Cue	Why?
High Ball (Figure 8.8)	Make a diamond, with thumbs pointing down. Ball fits into diamond.	Football makes a nice fit into the diamond
	Eyes focus on ball	Won't lose the ball. Better chance of hanging onto the ball.
Low Ball	Fingers collapse like a Venus flytrap	
	Elbows should act as a shock absorber. Quiet hands.	Ball does not bounce out of hands

Make a diamond with thumbs pointing down

Eyes focus on ball

Figure 8.8   Catching a Football

STRIKING—UNDERHAND SERVE

Skill	Cue	Why?
Hand Position	Palm up. Make a big palm. Or Palm up. Make a fist.	Bigger surface area for ball to contact; better control of ball
Foot Position [see also Chapter 18]	Step toward net with opposite foot of throwing arm	More power to the ball
	Arm close to body, brush shorts	Better efficiency
	Elbow straight	Helps with the follow-through
	Hit ball out of hand Like pitching horseshoes	Greater control of ball

STRIKING—OVERHAND SERVE

Skill	Cue	Why?
(Right-Handed Player)		
Stance	Stand sideways. Left foot forward points to target.	More power to serve and better weight transfer
Holding Ball [Figure 8.9]	Ball held in left hand in front of hitting shoulder	Allows for accurate hit. If ball is hit on the left side, will cause the hitting hand to be lower and ball will go into net.
Hitting Elbow	Hitting elbow up, like when using a bow and arrow	Keeps elbow high and ready to hit
Toss	Precise toss about 2 to 3 feet in front of hitting arm	Simplifies timing to contact ball
Hitting Action	Step, toss, hit the ball with heel of right hand	More surface area on the ball; better control
	Like throwing a football	
	Swing to target	

Hitting elbow up

Stand sideways, left
foot points to target

Ball held in left hand
in front of hitting
shoulder

Figure 8.9   Striking the Overhand Serve

Striking Activities

1. Serve against a wall first (emphasize hitting the ball hard).
2. If you have a net, start up close and work back.
3. Serve to partners over a lowered net. Gradually move the net higher.
4. Work on serving with right and left hands.

Mini-Games: Mini-Volleyball Tennis

KICKING/RECEIVING A PUNT

Skill	Cue	Why?
Kicking a Punt (Figure 8.10)	Hold ball with two hands, away from body	Ball is more stable
	Drop the ball	Less chance for error
	Support leg plants at the same time as dropping the ball	
(see also Chapter 11)	Pull back kicking leg	More power to send the ball far
	Swing leg under body	More effective technique
	Ball makes contact with shoelaces. Toes pointed down	More surface area on which to contact ball
	Follow-through: kick high	Gives greater distance to ball
Receiving a Punt		
Elbows	Five-point (hand-hand-elbow-elbow-bottom of sternum)	Big area for ball to land
	Make a cage with arms	More surface area for catching ball
	Fingers pointing to sky	Ball does not hurt the fingers
	Palms toward face Elbows to stomach	Place for ball to go
Action of Catching	Pull ball toward body	Ball won't drop to ground

Pull kicking leg back

Hold ball with two hands away from body

Support leg plants at the same time as dropping ball

Figure 8.10   Punting

Chapter 9

Basketball

Everyone likes to shoot baskets and dribble a ball. Some students spend hours just shooting the ball. We encourage students to practice shooting for many hours. When you teach this unit, we urge you to provide every student with a ball. The critical skills that students should learn are ball handling, dribbling, passing, and shooting. Provide many opportunities to dribble, pass, and shoot. Most of all, make basketball fun.

SKILLS LISTED WITH CUES

This chapter presents teaching cues and drill progressions for the following skills: ball-handling cues and drills, dribbling cues and drills, two-ball dribbling drills, passing and catching cues and drills, running and passing drills, three-man player drills, shooting cues and drills, lay-ups, free throw cues and drills, jumping, jump shot, rebounding, pick, off-ball defense, spacing, and man-to-man defense.

EQUIPMENT TIPS

1. One basketball for each student
2. If possible, baskets at different heights in the gym or outside
3. Stop watches
4. Colored vests
5. Scoreboard

TEACHING IDEAS

1. Every player must have a basketball.
2. To be proficient, students need to be able to dribble, pass, and shoot.
3. A goal is that everyone should be able to dribble, pass, and shoot with proficiency and control.
4. Practice, practice, practice! Encourage your students to practice outside of school time.
5. Dribbling, passing, and shooting with two balls helps develop ball-handling skills and coordination.
6. Know what the ball can do for you.

TEACHING PROGRESSIONS

The chapter provides great teaching progressions and drills in the cue section.

MINI-GAMES

1. Play a lot of half-court mini-games: 2 on 2, 3 on 3, 4 on 4, and 5 on 5.
2. Provide opportunities for students to practice handling the ball with their right and left hands in activities such as dribble tag, passing games, and shooting contests.
3. Be creative in games. Allow students to display their imaginations.
4. Use lower baskets to have a dunk contest. This helps students learn the basketball fundamentals of jumping, ball handling, court awareness, and decision making.
5. Time players on dribbling the length of the court. Teach right- and left-hand crossover, backwards, and so forth, when they are proficient with dribbling.
6. Time players when they rebound and throw a baseball pass to a teammate.
7. Have students make up a ball-handling routine—for example, around the head, around the waist, figure 8, dribble figure 8, and so forth.

FYI

Summer Camp:

Pat Summitt's Basketball Summer Camp
Tennessee Lady Vols Coaching Notebook
University of Tennessee
Knoxville, TN 37922
Phone: (423) 974-2866

BALL-HANDLING

Skill	Cue	Why?
Hand Position Drill	Slap the ball with wide fingers	This will develop a feel for the ball and control of the ball
Around the World	Move the ball around the waist; change directions, then move the ball around your head; then change directions	To develop quick reaction time with hands and body awareness
Figure 8 around Legs	Move ball in figure 8 formation around the knees and then change directions	
Scissor Walk with Basketball (Crab Walk) (Figure 9.1)	Lunging down the court, move the basketball in and out of your legs, going from baseline to baseline Big lanes on ball Head-up	Promote basketball position and coordination in ball movement

Head up

Big hands on the ball

Lunge down the court

Figure 9.1   Scissor Walk

FULL- AND HALF-COURT DRIBBLING DRILLS

Skill	Cue	Why?
Hand Placement on Ball When Dribbling	Thumb out, fingers spread wide, ball touching all five fingerpads when dribbling; look up court	Develop feel for the ball
Hand Action	Yo-yo action with your hand on the ball; push ball hard Waving action with your hand Hand waving down at the ball **Note:** Use left and right hands equally when practicing	Develop feel for hand on ball and force in dribbling
Eyes	Eyes looking up the court for open players and for opportunities to pass, shoot, or drive; see the defenders, but don't look at them	To develop court awareness and player positions
Speed Drills		
Change of Speed, Crossover	Emphasize change of direction and change of speed; keep head up	To promote ball handling skills and ability
Five-Trip Dribble (Single-Ball)	Used to change your directions	Dribbling skill development
Speed Dribble	Quickly dribble down the court with right hand; dribble back with left hand	Control with speed
The Crossover	Take three dribbles with the right hand toward the sideline, lower the dribble and cross the ball over to the left hand knee high, then dribble toward the other sideline; use the crossover down to the baseline and back to the other baseline. In a zig-zag pattern.	Develop change of direction skills
Around the Back	Take three dribbles with the right hand toward the right sideline; bring the ball around your back to the other hand, then dribble toward the other sideline; go down and back	

FULL- AND HALF-COURT DRIBBLING DRILLS

Skill	Cue	Why?
Five-Trip Dribble (*cont'd*)		
Through the Legs	Take three dribbles with the right hand toward the right sideline; make sure the left foot is in front when you bounce the ball between your legs to change directions, then dribble with the left hand toward the left sideline, make sure your right foot is forward to change directions; go down and back	
Reverse Spin	Take three dribbles toward the right sideline; keep ball in your right hand and spin so your back shuts out your defender; switch the ball to the left hand, take three dribbles, and reverse spin again; go down and back	
Five-Trip Dribble (Two-Balls)	Use to change your directions	
Speed Dribble (Figure 9.2)	Dribble two balls to half-court and back	
The Crossover	Focus on dribbling with non-preferred hand	Helps improve confidence, creativity, and dribbling skills
	Repeat the single-ball crossover drill using two balls, to half-court and back	Develop advanced skills in dribbling
The Reverse Spin	Repeat the single-ball reverse-spin drill using two balls, to half-court and back	
Through the Legs	Repeat single-ball drill with two balls	
Around the Back	Repeat single-ball drill with two balls	

Thumb out, fingers
spread wide, ball touching
all five finger pads

Eyes looking
down the court

Focus on dribbling with
non-preferred hand

Figure 9.2   Dribble Two Balls

PASSING AND CATCHING

Skill	Cue	Why?
Passing **Two-Hand Chest Pass** [Figure 9.3]		
Hand Position	Two thumbs down behind the ball	For proper spin
Fingers	Spread fingers wide	For control
Eyes	Eyes focused on your target	For accuracy
Passing Action	Extend your arms like shooting horizontally, following through with thumbs down	For proper speed and accuracy
	Palms out at finish	
Catching [Figure 9.4]		
Hand and Finger Position	Big hands, wide fingers	To develop receiving skill
Catching Action	Reach out, pull the ball in, or suck the ball in like a vacuum; your nickname, "Hoover"	Prevent defense from stealing ball

Thumbs down behind the
ball, spread fingers wide

Extend arms

Follow-through
with thumbs
down, palms out

Figure 9.3 Two-Hand Chest Pass

Big hands,
wide fingers

Smother ball
with eyes

Reach out

Figure 9.4 Catching

PASSING AND CATCHING

Skill	Cue	Why?
Catching (*cont'd*)		
Eyes	Smother the ball with your eyes	To assure catching
Passing and Catching Drills		
Partner Passing (Figures 9.5, 9.6)	Face each other using one ball, one-hand push pass with your right hand and then your left hand; follow through each time	Like shooting a basketball only horizontally with right hand To pass around a defender; right side/left side
Target Passing	Throw to your partner's target (e.g., partner's shoulder, head, or hands); make a target on the wall when practicing by yourself	Like shooting a basketball only horizontally with left hand
Chest Pass and Bounce Pass Simultaneously	Both partners have a ball; one partner will two-hand chest pass while the other partner will bounce pass at the same time; then switch after a while	Develop advanced skills in passing
Pass with a Figure 8	Perform a figure 8 around your knees, then pass to your partner off the figure 8; keep the ball moving	Passing while on the move
Behind the Back Passing	Standing slightly sideways, bring ball behind the back, pass to your partner; use your right hand, then your left hand	Alternative pass for advanced players
	Pass to wall behind your back	
Baseball Pass	Throw (as a football quarterback passes a football) to your partner	For long distance passing with accuracy
	Start close to your partner, then keep taking steps farther back, as needed, to throw farther	
	Stretch arm back and make an L at the elbow	
	Release the ball at 2:00 on your pretend clock	

Like shooting a basketball, only horizontally with right hand

Figure 9.5 One-Hand Push Pass with Right Hand

Like shooting a basketball, only horizontally with left hand

Figure 9.6 One-Hand Push Pass with Left Hand

PASSING AND CATCHING

Skill	Cue	Why?
One-Bounce Baseball Pass	Use strong and weak hands to throw your baseball passes with a bounce first Step farther back, as needed, to throw longer passes	Alternative pass for advanced players
Buzzer-Beater Baseball Pass Length of the Floor	Dribble once, then throw down court to partner at the other end of court, counting to self . . . 3–2–1 BZZZZZ	Develop end of game confidence
Two-Player Running and Passing Drills		
Dribbler and Trailer Full Court	Player 1 baseball passes to player 2, who is at half court Player 2 passes to player 1, who drives to the basket	To develop necessary skills in passing for advanced players
Pass and Cut Half-Court	Partner 1 stands at half-court Partner 2 stands on free-throw line, extended at the wing spot Partner 1 then passes to the wing and cuts hard inside to the basket, receiving the ball from partner 2 for a lay-up shot	

PASSING AND CATCHING

Skill	Cue	Why?
Three-Man Player Drills		
Three-Man Weave	Start with three lines, ball in middle line	To include movement in passing as done in game situations
	Running down court, middle passes to player on right side, who passes to the player coming toward him	
	Pass and go behind	
	Follow your pass	
	Be ready to receive ball back quickly	
	Person who receives the ball at key drives in for the lay-up	
	Use game speed	
	Go all out	
Side Center Side	Start with three lines, ball in middle line	
	Pass back and forth with no weave	
	Pass back and forth down court with one shooter	
	Perfect execution for the lay-up	
Rebound Pass	Two players start in the paint, one outside the paint	To develop fast break strategy
	Teacher tosses the ball off the rim	
	Player rebounds	
	Everyone takes off down court, with no dribble	
	Pass down the floor to closest player by the basket for the lay-up	
	We want to move the ball up the floor as quickly as possible for a quick lay-up	

SET SHOT

Skill	Cue	Why?
Set-Up	Shooting is the most important aspect of the game	To develop a knowledge base
	Two shots you must make are lay-ups and free throws; these are freebies	
	The best 3-point shot is a lay-up and free throw, not the arch shot	
Shooting Hand	Air valve between index finger and middle finger	To develop proper position for successful shooting
	Extend thumb along seam when shooting	
	Spread fingers	
	Hand up; balance like a waiter's tray	
(Figure 9.7, page 102)	Elbow makes an L, with ball sitting on a pretend serving tray of fingerpads	For proper angle and release
Nonshooting Hand	Hand faces side of ball; fingers only touch ball	
	Hand brushes ball	
Alignment	Arm, eye, and hand line up with nail hole in floor and with basket, like throwing a dart	
Sight	Focus on 2 inches above the rim	You have to see what your shooting for
	Basket looks like big bin, and the basket gets bigger on a good night—Michael Jordan	
Legs	Slightly bend knees, with buttocks out	Strength of shot comes from legs
Footwork	Feet square to basket and balanced	

Spread fingers

Elbow makes an "L" and points to basket

Hand up, balance like a waiter's tray

Figure 9.7   Shooting Hand with L (Hand Position)

SET SHOT

Skill	Cue	Why?
Shooting Action		
Fingers	Ball rolls off fingers for a nice, pretty backspin	To develop proper backspin
Wrist	Flip wrist, wave good-bye to ball	
Shoot Over	Shoot up over a telephone booth	Important for arch development
Path of Ball	Make a rainbow; exaggerate your arch, your first couple of shots	
Finish Position		
Wrist (Figure 9.8)	Gooseneck finish; thumb points at shoes	To ensure proper and consistent release
	Freeze hand at the top	
	Everything stays in a straight line (arm extended)	

Arm extended, everything stays in a straight line

Thumb points at shoes

Figure 9.8   Goose Neck Finish

FUNDAMENTAL SHOOTING DRILLS

Skill	Cue	Why?
Fundamental Drills		
Right Hand and Left Hand	Start close to the basket, shooting five on the right side one-handed, then shooting five on the left side one-handed	Develop confidence and form at close distances
Shooting Practice with No Defender	Take five steps back from under the basket: shoot five right-handed and five left-handed	Develop consistency and accuracy
	Take five steps back until you are at the free-throw line: shoot five with both hands	
Consecutive Free Throw	Consecutive free-throw shot with no dribble and a partner	Confidence
	Find a rhythm	

FUNDAMENTAL SHOOTING DRILLS

Skill	Cue	Why?
Fundamental Drills (*cont'd*)		
Shooter Rebounds Free Throw	Shooter rebounds ball before it touches floor and passes back to partner for the shot; so shooter rebounds own shot and passes to partner on foul line	Shoot and follow shot
	Left hand comes off ball with the shot; thus it is a one-handed shot	
	You want to shoot without a defender because you make more shots when you're open; when you're defended you tend to pass and not shoot	Shoot when open; more shots are made
Body Position for the Shot	Feet and hand must be in line with the basket; shoulders square	Extremely important for successful shooting
Three-Man Drills	You need a passer, shooter, and rebounder	Practice advanced skills
	Rebounder cannot let ball hit the floor before passing it to the passer	
	The passer bounce-passes it to the shooter along free-throw line	
	Shoot from the right side of the court and then the left side of the court, then rotate	
	Rebounder to passer to shooter to rebounder	
Three-Man Drill	Same formations as before, only the shooter runs along the 3-point line; he shoots where he receives the pass	

FUNDAMENTAL SHOOTING DRILLS

Skill	Cue	Why?
Fundamental Drills (*cont'd*)		
Two-Man Drill	Need a shooter and a rebounder	To develop individual shooting skills
	The shooter rebounds, passes to the partner, and plays defense on the shooter	
	Do not block the shot	
Three-Man Weave with a Bounce Pass	Get into three lines along the baseline, ball in the middle line	
	While running full court, pass the ball with a bounce pass to the right side; follow the pass and go behind	
	Expect the ball back	

LAY-UPS

Skill	Cue	Why?
Right-Handed		
The Approach	Head up, eyes focus on top of square	The closer you are to the basket, the more likely you are to make it
	Ball in outside hand with low approach	
	Step right, left, hop (jump)	
Release of Lay-up (Figure 9.9)	Bring ball close to chin; chin ball, step, and push off foot opposite shooting hand	Harder to block
	Extend shooting arm, reach high (ball kisses backboard)	
	Release ball at peak of reach	
	Soften shot because of speed	
	Get back for rebounding position	
Left-Handed (Figure 9.10)		
Footwork	Step left, right, hop (jump)	Same as right hand
Shooting Action	Left hand shoots ball	

Extend shooting
arm, reach high

Head up, eyes
focus on top
of square

Push off foot
opposite
shooting hand

Figure 9.9 Right-Handed
Lay-Up

Extend shooting
arm, reach high

Head up, eyes
focus on the
top of square

Push off foot
opposite
shooting hand

Figure 9.10 Left-Handed
Lay-Up

BASIC BALL-HANDLING

Skill	Cue	Why?
Ready Position	"Triple threat" Purpose: to fake out opponent with the option of the following skills: shooting, passing, dribbling	A position that allows player to execute all parts of game
Hand Position	Shooting position on ball	
Holding Ball	Hold ball to side on hip Keep ball on hip—hold ball to side to pass, dribble, or step into shot Elbows out	

FREE THROW

Skill	Cue	Why?
Front Toe Stays on Line	Work off the center of free-throw line, with front toe in direct line with rim	It lines up the player with the center of the basket
	Place front toe directly on center of free-throw line; find the nail hole	Shooting is a straight line function
	Put the front toe on same place every time; toe on the line	Consistency
Head Position	Put head down; head comes up with ball in one motion	Focuses eyes on target
	Head level, eyes up	
Balance	Get balanced on free-throw line	Important to have weight properly distributed
Routine	University of Tennessee uses player's choice—no dribble or one, two, or three dribbles	Develop consistency
Body	Body makes a line with the basket, same place every time	
Leg Action	Bend your knees, legs compel the shot	Consistency comes from the legs
Back Foot	Feet shoulder-width apart, then place back foot slightly back	Help maintain balance
	Back foot does not have anything to do with shot	
Fundamental Drills	Repetition and competition: dribble three, shoot	Develops confidence and consistency
	Rebounder passes to shooter	
	Find a rhythm	
	Example: Partner shooting: shoot five; one with the most made shots wins	
	Group free throw: everybody shoots one and runs for the missed shots	

FREE THROW

Skill	Cue	Why?
Fundamental Drills (*cont'd*)	Speed or lightning shots with eyes closed (Michael Jordon drill)	Advance skill players only
	More shots made off bounce shot—Why?	
	Body, legs are down; eyes are down—ready to go	

JUMP SHOT

Skill	Cue	Why?
Execution (Figure 9.11)	Jump above the defense, then shoot at the top of the jump; get high	Reduce blocked shots
	Body in a coil, all ready to jump	Develop consistency

Shoot at the top of the jump

Get high

Figure 9.11   Jump Shot

REBOUNDING

Skill	Cue	Why?
Attacking Basket	Work on blocking out, then attacking the basket	To reduce chance of opponent getting ball
One Player	Cover the weak side of basket (opposite side of shot)	70 percent of missed shots fall away from side shot on
	Most shots go long off the back side	
	Rebounding involves contact	
	Move from side to side and back up into a player; keep contact	
	Be active, aggressive, and alert	
Two Players	Check the player without the ball: if he moves to the basket take him; if not, attack the basket for the ball	To reduce chance of opponent getting ball

JUMPING AND DUNKING

Skill	Cue	Why?
Jumping		
Fundamentals	Jump naturally	Forged movement reduces mobility
	Work on getting high; act like a bungee cord	
Dunking	Lower baskets for student to dunk on	Develop confidence and have fun
	Practice dunking while working on jumping	
	Have lots of baskets to jump with	
	Use jump ropes	

BLOCKING OUT

Skill	Cue	Why?
Action of Body	Find with hands	Develop a routine to keep opponent from getting ball
	Wide stance	
Turn Back to Opponent	Put buttocks under opponent's hip—or sit on them or create a stable wall between opponent and ball	
Hands (after Pivot) (Figure 9.12)	Elbows out, palms wide; feel for opponent	

Elbows out, palms wide, feel for opponent

Buttocks out and sit on them

Wide stance

Figure 9.12   Blocking Out

THE PICK

Skill	Cue	Why?
Hustle	Earn your position	As to not foul
Stance	Stand wide	Develop larger target, more effective
	Weight on balls of feet	
Arms	Elbow bent and big	
Men	Hands clasped in front to protect sensitive parts of your body	
Women	Arms crossed against body to protect sensitive parts of your body	
Coming Off the Pick	Rub shoulder to shoulder	To shake off the defender with the pick
	Right to right	
	Left to left	
Pick and Roll	After you pick, you pivot toward basket	Gives a player more opportunity to get open
	Hand up high; ask for ball	
	Receive pass and go in for lay-up or shot	
Defender Going through a Pick	Anticipate; take a hook step around player	To beat the defender to a position

OFFENSIVE FOOTWORK

Skill	Cue	Why?
Technique	Read and triple-threat position	To develop advanced skills
	Two-step stop–emphasize on heel–toe (jump stop to be used for post people only)	
	Change of speed and direction	
	Shot fake and drive—left and right (without the ball)	

OFFENSIVE ONE-ON-ONE MOVES

Skill	Cue	Why?
Guards and Wings	Catch and shoot	To develop confidence and advanced skills
	Catch and drive	
	Catch and reverse	
	Catch shot fake and drive	
	Catch, swing through, and drive	
	Catch, jab, and go (emphasis on heel–toe technique)	
Posts	Front pivot shot (both ways)	
	Front pivot crossover	
	Drop step baseline/power shot	
	Drop step middle, drophook, jumphook, or power shot	
	Pull back-shot drive	
	Post people can also use perimeter drills	

SPACING

Skill	Cue	Why?
Teach Spacing When Passing on Offense		
Spacing Creates Open Areas (Figures 9.13A & B)	The perfect passing distance is 15 feet	Put pressure on defense to react
	Anything beyond 15 feet is a potential stolen pass	
	Teach students to play off each other to create efficient spacing	
	Use the free-throw line to gauge distance; use lines on the floor to gauge the distance of 15 feet	

Pass the ball within 15 feet

Any pass longer than 15 feet potentially may be stolen

Figure 9.13A   Fifteen-Foot Pass—Offensive Player

Eyes on the player you are guarding and then eyes on the ball switch back and forth

Pistol formation—Point to opponent, point to ball

Figure 9.13B   Pistol—Defensive Player

DEFENSE

Skill	Cue	Why?
Man-to-Man Defense	Force opponents from the middle to the sideline; force them to play on one side of the floor	So team mates will know where to help
On-Ball Defense (Figure 9.14)	One hand is under the ball or mirrors the ball, the other hand is in the passing lane	Prepares defender to block pass or steal ball
Help Defense (see Figure 9.13B)	Deny defense; one hand always in the passing lane, palm facing ball	Develops a team defense concept
	Eyes on the player you're guarding, then eyes on the ball two passes away in pistol formation	

One hand is under the ball

One hand is in the passing lane

Figure 9.14   On-Ball Defense

Chapter 10

Floor Hockey

Floor hockey is a fast sport because of its transitions, that players are constantly moving from offense to defense, and the speed of the puck or ball. You can substitute players during play without waiting for a whistle. Students have more playing time. Floor hockey develops cardiovascular endurance, core strength, reaction time, hand–eye coordination, foot speed, and agility. Floor hockey also works on skills that transfer to other sports, such as soccer and lacrosse.

Floor hockey is a sport that can be played successfully by all students. There is a role for every student, regardless of physical stature. Each student's personality plays a major role in the cohesion of the team.

SKILL LISTED WITH CUES

This chapter focuses on cues for the following skills: stance, grip, stick position, forehand passing, backhand passing, forehand receiving, backhand receiving, shooting, and goaltending.

EQUIPMENT TIPS

1. Sticks that have a plastic or wood shaft should be used.
2. A plastic puck is recommended for safety reasons because it is easy to control and harder to lift. A plastic ball also works well.
3. PVC nets are recommended for safety and durability instead of metal nets, if you have an option.
4. Safety equipment for all players includes helmet with face mask, gloves, shin guards that cover from the ankles to the top of the knee, and a mouth guard.
5. The goalie needs a helmet with face mask, catcher and blocker gloves, and shin guards.
6. Colored vests should be worn to identify the teams.

TEACHING IDEAS

1. Teach the players to keep the sticks on the floor at all times. This prevents high sticks, causing possible injury. If a player breaks the sticks on the floor rule during a game, that player sits out for 2 minutes, just like in ice hockey. The team plays one player short for the duration of the penalty.
2. Teach the players to watch out for each other. They should avoid hitting another player's ankles, tangling up sticks, or causing a player to fall.
3. Make sure players are in a good hockey stance, stick on floor, knees slightly bent, like making a triangle with stick and feet. Emphasize good posture while in the sitting position: head over shoulders, shoulders over hips, hips over heels.
4. When teaching passing and shooting, make sure to teach the transfer of weight from the back leg to the forward leg. This increases the power of the shot and helps with the accuracy of the follow-through.
5. When teaching passing and shooting, emphasize the wrist roll-over during the follow-through. When executed properly, the blade of the stick faces down toward the floor. The stick should point to the target and be a foot or so off the floor.

TEACHING PROGRESSIONS

1. When practicing accuracy, have the students stand 10 to 15 feet from a wall. Each student will pick a spot on the wall or have a target at which to aim, for example, a cone. Having a target helps the student focus on rolling the wrist over and pointing toward the target with the stick.
2. Have students stand 20 feet apart with a partner. Work on passing and receiving skills. When students can do this with control, move the partners closer together and have them speed up the passes. The goal of this drill is to improve passing accuracy, receiving speed, and the releasing of a pass.
3. Hang a vest in the upper corners of the goal and/or place cones on the floor in the lower corners. Have three to four students stand in a semicircle. Have each student shoot for the vests. This improves shot accuracy, speed, and power (Figure 10.1)

Students shoot for the vests

Hang vests in upper corners of the goal

Figure 10.1 Shooting Drill

MINI-GAMES

Play games of 3 on 3, 4 on 4, or 5 on 5. Set up several mini-games using the width of a basketball court. If a team scores 3 points, it stays on the court, and the opponents step off the court. The next team of three comes onto the court and plays a new game. These games keep the players moving. You can also play these games with goalies at each end.

FLOOR HOCKEY RULES AND GAME

- Due to the physical nature of the game, it is important to abide by a set of rules. Enforcing these rules keeps the sport safe and the game in control.
- If a player breaks a rule, send him to the 2-minute penalty box.
- Slashing (using a stick to strike another player) is a violation.
- Tripping (using a stick, knee, foot, arm, hand, or elbow to cause an opponent to trip or fall) is a violation.
- *High-sticking* is carrying the stick above the shoulders.
- Interference with the progress of an opponent who is not in possession of the puck or ball is a violation.
- Unsportsmanlike conduct, such as an overly violent behavior, swearing, teasing, fighting, and so forth, is a violation.
- Cross-checking—when a player has both hands on her stick (off the ground) and uses the stick to shove another player—is a violation.

HOCKEY STANCE		
Skill	**Cue**	**Why?**
Feet (Figure 10.2)	Slightly wider than shoulder width, flat and firm on floor	Stability, balance, ready to move forward, backward, or laterally
Knees	Slightly bent, but not over toes	Stability, balance, ready to move forward, backward, or laterally
Hips	Slightly back	Core stability and balance Helps knees from going over toes
Stomach/Back	Keep stomach muscles tight and back straight	For core stability
Head	Head up. Looking forward over entire floor.	Allows you to see entire floor and what is happening
Holding Stick	Arms in front, holding stick straight out, forming a triangle with feet and stick	Stability, balance, ready for pass
	Stick blade flat on ground 2–3 feet in front of feet	More surface area on ground to hit puck

Emphasize These Cues

1. Feet firm on floor
2. Hips slightly back
3. Back straight, head up
4. Stick flat on floor; form a triangle with feet

Form a triangle with feet and stick

Knees slightly bent, not over toes

Figure 10.2 Hockey Stance

GRIPS		
Skill	**Cue**	**Why?**
Right-Hand Shot	Left hand on top; right hand halfway down shaft	Left hand is power hand Right hand is control hand
Left-Hand Shot	Right hand on top; left hand halfway down shaft	Right hand is power hand Left hand is control hand
Top Hand	Form a V with thumb and index finger; place at the top of shaft	
Bottom Hand	Form a V with thumb and index finger; place about halfway down shaft	Good control of stick Able to utilize more power
Knuckles of Each Hand	Knuckles of each hand will face opposite direction of each other	Good control. Hand halfway down the shaft utilizes flex in stick for harder and faster shot.

STICK HANDLING

Skill	Cue	Why?
Stick Position	Hold stick in front of body, forming a triangle with feet and blade	Balance, stability, ready for puck pass
	Blade should be flat on floor 2–3 feet in front of feet	
Stick-Handling Stance		
Stance	Good hockey stance	
Head	Head up. See puck in peripheral vision.	Can see the rest of floor and action going on
Stick Motion	Blade travels parallel to foot line	Control of puck
	Blade rotates toward puck at about 45-degree angle	
	Blade "cups" puck and pulls puck forward and backward	Control of puck
Wrists	Wrists roll toward puck when you catch puck	Control of puck

Emphasize These Cues

1. Keep puck between feet (stick on outside of puck); thus you have to pick up blade and place on other side of puck. Do this while rolling wrists to get 45-degree angle.
2. Use soft hands; there should be noise from the puck hitting the stick.

FOREHAND PASSING

Skill	Cue	Why?
Stance	Good hockey stance	
Puck Position (Figure 10.3)	Puck starts at heel of blade and behind back foot. Travels forward to toe of blade and then off blade.	Gives proper spin on puck Control
	Puck travels parallel to foot line	Accuracy, power, and speed of pass
Stick	Puck stays on floor	Accuracy, ease of receiving pass
	Sweep puck parallel to foot line	
	Puck is released from blade slightly in front of front foot.	

Puck starts at heel of blade

Left hand on top, right hand half-way down shaft

Figure 10.3   Passing and Shooting Position

FOREHAND PASSING		
Skill	**Cue**	**Why?**
Stick (*cont'd*)	Hands on top of stick and halfway down shaft	
	Blade "cups" puck throughout motion	
	Blade should end up 1–2 feet above floor, with blade pointing toward floor	
Head and Eyes	Look at puck position on blade, look at target, look at puck position, pass	
Wrists	Follow puck path to its receiver	Improves follow-through keeps pass down
	As you sweep puck forward, roll wrist forward toward target	Puts proper spin on puck, keeps puck down

Emphasize These Cues

1. Weight on back foot (see Figure 10.4A)
2. Puck starts at heel of blade
3. Blade sweeps puck forward, with a cupping motion
4. See target, then puck, and pass
5. Roll wrist toward target

BACKHAND PASSING

Skill	Cue	Why?
Backhand Passing	This motion is the same as the forehand pass. Reverse the motion. Puck starts on back foot Weight on back foot Transfer weight to front foot	

FOREHAND RECEIVING

Skill	Cue	Why?
Stance (Figure 10.4B)	Good hockey stance	
Head and Eyes	Watch puck come all the way in to blade until you have control of puck	Ensures you receive puck and maintain control
Stick Position	Stick path parallel to foot line	Control
	Blade flat on floor, slightly in front of foot	Greater area on floor to receive pass, more time to catch pass
	When puck reaches blade, pull blade backward to absorb pass	
	Blade travels all the way back to back foot	Control
	Blade cups puck as it moves backward	Control
Puck Position	Initial catch is on toe of blade (front third of blade) As you absorb puck, it should travel forward with heel of blade	Control and allows for immediate pass or shot because puck is in proper position
Wrist Position	Wrists roll forward for in-coming pass, as stick and hands absorb the pass	Control. Soft hands to help absorb pass. Wrists in position to immediately pass or shoot.

Emphasize These Cues

1. Hockey stance
2. Watch puck into stick blade
3. Absorb puck with blade in a reverse sweeping motion
4. Roll wrist forward when puck meets blade

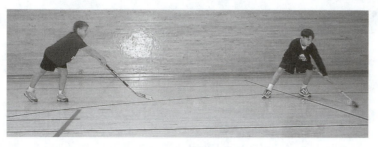

Blade sweeps puck forward with a cupping motion

Roll wrist toward target

Figure 10.4A   Passing to a Partner

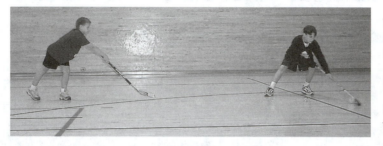

Watch puck come all way into blade

Blade flat on floor

Pull blade backward to absorb pass

Figure 10.4B   Receiving a Pass

BACKHAND RECEIVING

Skill	Cue	Why?
Backhand Receiving	This motion is the same for a forehand or backhand pass reception. Reverse motion.	
	As puck approaches, weight should be on front foot. As you absorb puck with stick and hands, transfer weight to back foot.	This makes you ready to immediately pass again or shoot

SHOOTING

Skill	Cue	Why?
Forehand Wrist Shot (Figure 10.5)	Bottom hand on stick should slide 2–3 inches further down	
	Weight transfer is very important. Drive off back leg.	Use of legs and hips aids speed and power of shot
	Sweeping motion of stick should be faster than a pass	
	Bend knees a little more	To add in weight transfer while keeping good hockey stance
	Roll wrists over and point blade at target	
	Height of follow-through affects height of shot	

SHOOTING

Skill	Cue	Why?
Backhand Wrist Shot	Same cues as for forehand wrist shot. Reverse motion. Momentum from weight transfer should "pull" shooter onto the front foot only	

Bottom hand should slide 2 to 3 inches further down stick

Sweeping motion of stick should be faster than a pass

Roll wrists over and point blade at target

Figure 10.5   Shooting

Emphasize These Cues

1. Good stance
2. Lower hand slides 2 to 3 inches down shaft
3. Transfer weight from back foot to front foot
4. Roll wrists over and point blade at target

GOALTENDING

Skill	Cue	Why?
Stance (Figure 10.6)	Head over shoulders, shoulders over hips, hips over ankles, feet shoulder-width apart. Bend knees at 45-degree angle.	Having good posture allows quick reaction time to stop the ball or puck
Hand Position	Hold open catching hand off to the side, waist level	Having the open hand off to the side takes up more space, protecting the net even more. It also keeps the hand ready to respond quicker
	The opposite hand holds the stick so the blade is on the ground in front and makes triangle with feet Blade flat on the ground	Having the stick on the ground in front of the feet provides a barrier between the feet so that the puck does not get past It also protects more surface area of the net

Emphasize These Cues

1. Hockey stance
2. Catching hand open, up waist-high, and off to side
3. Stick blade flat on floor, making a triangle with feet

Catching hand open, off to side

Blade and feet make a triangle

Blade flat on ground

Figure 10.6   Goalie Stance

Note

1. The goaltender is the last line of defense. The goaltender has one major goal: to stop the puck. The most effective way of goaltending is to take up as much area of the goal plane as possible. The goaltender's body and the stick help to take up this area.

2. To avoid muscle pulls and strains, always make sure that the goaltenders and players are properly stretched before any activity begins. Goaltenders need to be flexible, because the position requires a quick reflex time, which could cause injury if the player is not warmed up properly.

3. Before beginning the game, let the goaltender's team take practice shots, from a distance, at the goaltender. This drill serves the important role of getting the goaltender's reflex time prepared for scrimmage, as well as warming up the rest of the team.

Chapter 11

Football

When teaching flag football, keep the rules as close to those of the regular game as possible. The students can relate to our national pastime easier. Football is a huge part of our society. The students will be able to enjoy the game with their family or friends because they will know the skills, rules, and some common plays.

SKILLS LISTED WITH CUES

The cues in this chapter cover the following skills: throwing, catching, punting, catching a punt, snapping the ball, quarterback steps, lateral pass, hand-offs (right and left side), tuck away after catch, running down the sideline, blocking, and in, out, and post running routes.

EQUIPMENT TIPS

1. New Tech Tac footballs have an easy web grip. Two sizes are available: 6-inch and mini-footballs. Nerf multicolor footballs and Zwirl footballs are easy to grip and throw, or you may use smaller leather footballs. Avoid using large, regulation-size leather balls, as they are difficult to throw and catch. See the FYI section for information on ordering these fun balls.
2. Order a variety of colored vests: red, yellow, green, orange, purple, and blue.
3. Flags with Velcro belts: This avoids the question of whether the player was down.
4. Flip scorecards: If players can see a scorecard, it will add motivation to the game.
5. For those who play recreation and league football, use a helmet, pads, and rubber cleats (Figure 11.1).

Helmet

Pads

Figure 11.1
Practice Equipment

Rubber cleats

TEACHING IDEAS

Divide students into pairs: a highly skilled student with one with fewer skills. Have them practice the skills together. The highly skilled student can give tips to the other one.

TEACHING PROGRESSIONS

1. Practice throwing a football with the right and left hands. Play Throwbee.
2. Practice kicking a football with the right foot and the left foot. Play Philadelphia Football.
3. Practice catching a punted ball with a partner. Challenge the pair to catch 10, 15, or 20 balls.
4. Practice plays with three players. One is the center, one is the quarterback, and one is the receiver. Rotate positions after three thrown balls. Teach the quarterback steps and centering skills. Add a defender and teach the defensive skill of back peddling and mirroring the offensive player.
5. Play 4 on 4 (passing plays only).
6. Practice hand offs and a lateral pass. Play 3 on 3 mini-games with running plays only.
7. Practice a combination of passing and running plays.
8. Let the teams make up their own play patterns and play 4 on 4 games.

MINI-GAMES

1. Throwbee with a football (see Chapter 8)
2. Philadelphia Football (see Chapter 8)
3. Mini-games of 2 on 2 and 3 on 3: These games can be played to practice in, out, and post plays, with a defender on each player.

MODIFIED FLAG FOOTBALL RULES

1. Six to eight players on a team
2. Football field, using 40 to 50 yards for each mini-game
3. Kick off from the 20 yard line
4. Each team has four plays to make a touch down. Why? Players don't have to worry about keeping track of the line of scrimmage.
5. Score the game just like a regulation football game.

   6 points for a touchdown
   1 point for a run-in after the touchdown
   2 points for a pass-in after the touchdown
   2 points for a safety. A safety is occurs when the defensive team pulls the flag off an offensive player who is in their offensive end zone (safety zone is 3 yards).

6. Any offensive player on the line can catch the pass.
7. There is a 3-yard neutral zone. The students take three steps back from the line of scrimmage. The line of scrimmage is where the football lays.
8. A lateral pass is the same as in regulation football. The pass must be thrown behind the quarterback or to the side. There are no forward lateral passes.
9. The quarterback must be behind the line of scrimmage in order to throw a forward pass.
10. In this game, no one is standing around. Everyone is moving and having fun practicing all the skills. If you have a class of 32 students, you could organize four mini-games, with four players on each team.

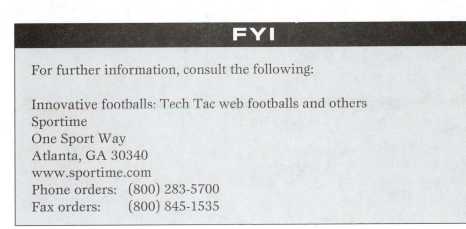

FYI

For further information, consult the following:

Innovative footballs: Tech Tac web footballs and others
Sportime
One Sport Way
Atlanta, GA 30340
www.sportime.com
Phone orders: (800) 283-5700
Fax orders: (800) 845-1535

THROWING

Skill	Cue	Why?
Grip	Grab top of ball like holding a soda pop can or a fish's head	More surface area on ball, better control
	Put three to four fingers on the laces, depending on the size of your hand	Better grip
	Fingerpads hold laces	
Throwing Action [Figure 11.2]	Stretch arm way back; make an L shape	For better control and to throw the ball farther
Stance and Leg Action	Short to medium step	To get rid of the football fast
Release Point	Release at 2:00 with right hand; left hand, 10:00. Football points upward.	Ball will go at correct angle
Follow-Through Action	Turn palm out on follow-through. Ball comes off index finger.	Ball will fly through the air in a spiral motion

CATCHING

Skill	Cue	Why?
Hand Action [Figure 11.3]	Big hands. Reach out. Shape hands like a diamond	Won't bounce off chest
	Catch ball in diamond	Ball fits best
Eyes	Pull ball into chest; watch ball into chest	Helps to avoid dropping ball

Stretch arm way back, make an "L"

Finger pads hold laces

Short to medium step

Figure 11.2 Throwing

Shape hands like a diamond

Big hands, reach out

Figure 11.3 Catching

KICKING A PUNT		
Skill	**Cue**	**Why?**
Punting (Figure 11.4)	Hold ball with two hands away from body	Ball is more stable
	Drop the ball	Less chance for error
	Support foot plants at the same time as dropping the ball	
	Pull kicking leg back	More power to send the ball far
	Swing leg under body	More effective technique
	Ball makes contact with shoelaces and below knee. Toes pointed down.	More surface area on which to contact ball
Follow-Through (Figure 11.5)	Kick high, like a scissors kick	Gives more distance to ball

Swing leg
under body

Pull kicking
leg back

Figure 11.4   Punting

Kick high like
a scissor kick

Figure 11.5   Punting: Follow-Through

CATCHING A PUNT

Skill	Cue	Why?
Elbows (Figure 11.6)	5-point (hand–hand–elbow–elbow–bottom of sternum)	Big area for ball to land
	Make a cage with arms	More surface area to catch ball
	Fingers pointing to sky	Does not hurt the fingers
	Palms toward face	Place for ball to go
	Elbows to stomach	
Action of Catching	Pull ball toward chest	Ball won't drop to ground

SNAPPING BALL FROM THE SIDE

Skill	Cues	Why?
Foot Position to the Ball	Feet behind ball	A rule: feet behind the ball on line of scrimmage
Hand Position on the Ball	Hold top of ball with an eagle claw	More surface area on the ball, more control of ball
Hiking Action with the Arm	Straight arm to the quarterback	More accuracy with this method
	Put the ball into the quarterback's hands. Focus on hands.	Gives you a focus on the target
		More concentration and better accuracy

Fingers pointing to sky

Make a cage with arms

Elbows to stomach, pull ball to chest

Figure 11.6 Catching a Punted Ball

QUARTERBACK DROP BACK		
Skill	**Cue**	**Why?**
Foot Action	After receiving the snap, turn to side, and sidestep	These steps help the quarterback have a fast reaction time.
	Grapevine	
	Slide–slide	
	Plant your back foot and throw	The player has better control of the ball at the time of the throw

LATERAL PASS (A PITCH)

Skills	Cue	Why?
Hand Position	Hold ball with two hands	Better ball control
	Wide fingers on ball	More surface area on the ball, better control
Throwing Action (Figure 11.7)	Underhand throw	
	Arms straight	
	Aim for the number on the jersey	
Rule	Lateral pass has to go behind or to the side	A forward pass is illegal

Aim for number on jersey

Hold ball with two hands

Underhand throw, arms straight

Figure 11.7   Lateral Pass

HAND-OFFS

Skill	Cue	Why?
To Right Side of Quarterback		
Receiver Arm Position	Inside elbow up	Better target area for ball to go in
	Outside elbow down	
	Arms are parallel to each other	
Quarterback Action	Put the ball between the receiver's arms	Target place
Receiver Action	Squeeze the ball	Ball won't fall out
To Left Side of Quarterback [Figure 11.8]		
Receiver Arm Position	Inside elbow up	The ball fits in the pocket better
	Outside elbow down	
	Arms are parallel to each other	Elbow is not in the way
Quarterback Action	Put the ball between the receiver's arms	Target place
Receiver Action	Squeeze the ball	Ball won't fall out

Put ball between receiver's arms

Inside elbow up
Outside elbow down

Arms are parallel
and squeeze ball

Figure 11.8 Hand-Off

BALL-CARRYING TECHNIQUES

Skills	Cue	Why?
Tuck Away after Catch	Tuck ball into four REEF pressure points:	Ball won't get loose
Arm Action	**R**ib Cage (stuff ball into rib cage	Ball protected
	Elbow (tuck elbow in)	Holds the ball in place
	Eagle claw (spread fingers over point of ball)	Large surface area means more control of the ball
	Forearm (covers ball)	Holds ball against the body, so the ball won't bounce out
Running Down Sideline	SOAPS = **S**witch **O**utside **A**rm **P**osition	
Ball Position	Running to the right sideline, carry ball in right hand	If ball gets knocked out, the ball will roll out of bounds
	Running to the left sideline, carry ball in left hand	If ball gets knocked out, the ball will roll out of bounds

BLOCKING

Skill	Cue	Why?
Stance	Get into a comfortable squat position, as if you are sitting on a chair	
Arm Action	Arms crossed in front of body, ready to contact the defender	Quicker reaction time
	Feet shoulder-width apart	
Strategy	Keep the opponent away from the ball carrier	Keeps you on the opponent
Body Force	Push with your upper body, using your legs for strength and balance	Legal position on the block

BASIC RECEIVER ROUTES

Skill	Cue	Why?
In Route (Figure 11.9)	Run straight pivot to outside	To fake opponent
	Cut to middle: run a straight line to middle. Find an open area between defenders.	Get to ball faster and run away from opponent
	Big hands for target for the quarterback	More target area for the quarterback to see and the receiver to catch the ball
Out Route (Figure 11.10)	Run straight, pivot to inside, and cut to the outside. Run toward the sidelines. Find an open area between defenders.	To fake opponent
	Run a straight line	Get to ball faster
	Big hands, for the quarterback to have a target	More target area for the quarterback to see, and the receiver has more surface area in which to catch the ball
Post Route	Run straight for 10 to 12 yards, then cut to one of the goal posts	Fakes defender
Stop Route	Run straight	The defender will not know in what direction you will be going
	Stop as if you had come to a stop sign	The defender will be slow to react to your sudden movement
	Turn around, with your arms and hands ready to receive the ball	Provides a good target to receive the ball
Fly Route	Run straight until you pass the defender	The defender will not know where you are going
	Don't stop	Run away from the defender

Big hands
for target

Find an open area
between defenders

Cut to middle, run
a straight line

Figure 11.9   In Route

Run toward sideline,
run a straight line

Find an open area
between defenders

Figure 11.10   Out Route

Chapter 12

Quad Ball

Quad Ball is a new sport, with elements that enhance cardiovascular conditioning. The game is played by two teams on a basketball court with no out-of-bounds. There are five to eight players on each team. The game is played with a Nerf soccer ball. The game is called Quad Ball because it integrates four sports: soccer, speed-a-way, basketball, and football. Skill development appears to be accelerated when the students have the opportunity to practice a game that incorporates four different sports within the context of one game.

Quad Ball provides an opportunity for the students to think critically about how to effectively manipulate the ball to score points. Students also learn how to apply strategies in a variety of ways. The game provides opportunity for all students to score, opportunity to work on sportsmanship, maximum participation, and is adaptable for large classes.

Quad Ball was invented at Brigham Young University in a graduate methods class in 1988. One of the goals of the class was to design a game for a biomechanics instructional unit. Wooden pins were added as a scoring option. Wooden pins have been replaced by plastic tennis cans for safety.

Since its inception, Quad Ball has been played in numerous physical education and recreational settings. The sport has increased in popularity because of its unique characteristics, the options to score, the variety of athletic skills utilized, and the amount of cardiovascular fitness it offers.

EQUIPMENT TIPS

1. One or two Nerf or webb or foam soccer balls (Figure 12.1)
2. Twelve empty plastic tennis cans
3. Mesh vests to field one team
4. One whistle, one stopwatch
5. Scoreboard of some type
6. Designated time-out box

Web ball

Twelve empty tennis cans

Mesh vests

Scoring system

Nerf or foam balls

Figure 12.1   Quad-Ball Equipment

TEACHING IDEAS

1. Have two players demonstrate the scoring options.
2. Demonstrate aerial conversions.
3. Use four players to demonstrate an abbreviated version of the game while other players observe.
4. Add two players at a time until all members of each team are playing.
5. Stop play when rules are violated, and make corrections.
6. Rotate teams every 5 to 10 minutes so that large classes can play.
7. Players on the sideline can keep score, keep time, set up knocked down tennis cans, help officiate, and encourage other players.
8. Organize tournaments with teams from other physical education classes. Have teams keep score daily. Options for teams could be all girls, all boys, or coed teams.

SKILL PROGRESSIONS

1. Teach the skills in Chapter 8 on throwing, catching, and kicking. Teach the basic skills of basketball and soccer, then introduce your students to Quad Ball. A list of the skills used in Quad Ball are found in the section on cues.
2. Teach the five conversion skills found in the cue section.
3. We designed many of the skill progressions and drills found in the Quad Ball book. See the FYI section for more information.

QUAD BALL

Court

You will need one indoor basketball court or playing area that has four walls, curtains, or other dividers. The court or playing area needs a basketball hoop at each end and to be clear of all obstacles.

Teammate
behind
end-line

Player behind
free-throw line

Figure 12.2   Scoring: Throwing a Touchdown Pass

Scoring

There are three ways to score in Quad Ball: (1) throwing a touchdown pass from the free-throw line (1 point), the center line (2 points), the opponents' free-throw line (3 points), and baseline to baseline (4 points) (Figure 12.2); (2) shooting the ball into the basket from inside the key lane (1 point) (Figure 12.3), from outside the free-throw lane (2 points), from the 3-point line (3 points), and with

One point is scored if made
inside key

Figure 12.3   Scoring: Shooting inside the Key

One point scored for each can knocked over

Figure 12.4   Scoring: Knocking down Empty Tennis Cans

a slam dunk (4 points); and (3) knocking down the empty tennis cans while kicking or throwing the ball (1 point for each can) (Figure 12.4). Each player has many opportunities to be successful because of the variety of scoring options provided in the game.

Rules and Violations

1. *Soccer Center Kick:* The game is started with a soccer center kick from the center line. Each team must stay behind the center line until the ball is kicked. The ball must go forward 1 yard and touch another player. A free kick is taken from the point of violation.
2. *Converting a Ball to an Aerial Ball:* A ball on the ground may be converted to an aerial ball by a two-legged lift up, one foot lift to a teammate, one foot roll and lift to self, lifting a rolling ball to self, and catching the ball off the wall.
3. *Three-Step Rule:* Once the ball is aerial, a player is permitted to take three steps with the ball. A free kick is taken from the point of violation.
4. *Five-Second Rule:* A player is permitted to hold the ball 5 seconds before shooting or passing. A free kick is taken from the point of violation.
5. *Free Kick:* If a player commits a foul, such as pushing, tripping, kicking, elbowing, charging, blocking, holding, or striking, a free kick is awarded at the point of violation. Players must be 5 yards away from the ball before the ball is kicked.
6. *Flagrant Foul:* A *flagrant foul* is defined as attempting to hurt someone or performing a dangerous move in the game. When a flagrant foul is commit-

ted, a free kick is awarded at the point of the foul, and the player who committed the foul is removed from the game for 2 minutes.

7. *Picking the Ball off the Floor:* If the ball touches the gym floor and a player picks up the ball, a free kick is awarded to the opponent at the point of the violation.

8. *Touchdown Pass Rule:* If a player throws the ball from inside the foul line and a teammate catches the ball across the endline, no point is awarded for a touchdown. However, the player may attempt to knock over a tennis can.

Coed Rules

All the rules are the same, except for the following:

1. There are six to eight players on each team:
   Six-player teams have three boys and three girls.
   Eight-player teams have four boys and four girls.
   The number of girls can exceed the number of boys, but the number of boys cannot exceed the number of girls.

2. Boys should guard boys, and girls should guard girls. If a boy guards a girl, he must position himself 3 feet away from the girl. A violation of this rule will result in a free kick from the point of violation.

3. If any player knocks another player down, a free kick is awarded at the point of violation. If the violation is intentional, the player is removed from the game and stays in the time-out box for 2 minutes.

4. Scoring opportunities: Alternate girl, then boy.

Safety Guidelines

The following safety guidelines are highly recommended:

1. Make sure to use empty plastic tennis cans, to prevent injury.

2. Use a Nerf soccer ball, to prevent injury.

3. Train students to officiate the rules closely. Observe all of the rules, because of the high intensity of the game. There is no out-of-bounds to stop play, and play can get rough if the official does not closely call fouls and violations.

4. If players become rough, and to avoid injury, provide a time-out box for those students who do not obey the rules. During each lesson, review the risks that are involved. When possible, create teams that have equal skill levels.

MINI-GAMES

Inside Modifications

1. *Cardiac Bypass:* The ball can bounce once or twice (depending on the skill level of the players) before it is caught, to count as an aerial ball. This modification can be used for students in upper elementary grades and middle school. It can also be used as a teaching progression during the first few days of presenting Quad Ball.

2. *Cafeteria Quad Ball: Equipment:* Tape different sizes (large, medium, and small) of targets on the baseline walls.

   Play Quad Ball, with the exception of the following:

   Targets on the baseline walls are worth different points:

   1 point for large targets

   2 points for medium targets

   3 points for small targets

   A touchdown pass equals 1 point (ball is thrown from behind the half-court line to the baseline or other designated line, depending on class skill level)

   | Fourth grade | Play with two bounces |
   | Fifth and sixth grade | Play with one bounce |

3. *Side-Court Quad Ball:*

   Developed by: Brett Hansen, Jefferson Middle School, Preston, Idaho.

   Purpose: To utilize more court space and increase participation

   Equipment: An 8-inch sponge ball. This type of ball is more appropriate for a smaller court area.

   Floor space: Played on side basketball court. Use side baskets.

   Rules: If the ball goes over the middle sideline, use a soccer throw-in. All other Quad Ball rules apply.

4. *Super Quad Ball:* The game may be played using two balls. However, if two balls are used, there needs to be one official on each ball and one scorekeeper for each ball. A player may play either ball on the court. If one team scores, the official then gives the ball to the opposing team and a soccer throw-in is taken. The other ball continues in play.

Outside Modifications

1. *Cardiac Court Quad Ball:* This game is played on an outside basketball court. A soccer throw-in is taken when the ball goes out of bounds. All other rules apply.

2. *Pulse-a-Fire Quad Ball: Equipment:*

   A grass field

   Six 1-liter plastic soda bottles for each side. If it's windy, place a little sand in the bottom of each bottle.

   Two soccer goals

   One soccer ball (game could be played with two soccer balls)

   Rules: Use the same rules as for Quad Ball, with these exceptions:

   A soccer throw-in is taken where the ball goes out of bounds.

   Knocking a soda bottle over equals 1 point.

   A soccer ball kicked into a goal equals 2 points.

   Touchdown pass:

   10 yards from baseline equals 1 point

   20 yards from baseline equals 3 points

FYI

Fronske, H., Wilson, R., & Harrison, J. (1995). *Quad ball! A new aerobic sport.* Logan, UT: Utah State University.

Quad Ball book available (45 pages). Cost is $7.00, plus shipping:
Utah State University Bookstore
Logan, UT 84322-7000
Phone: (800) 662-3950

CONVERTING TO AN AERIAL BALL

Skill	Cue	Why?
Two-legged Lift (Figure 12.5)		
Foot Position on Ball	Feet are like pliers; squeeze ball between feet	Ball will stay between feet
Jumping Action	Turn heels to outside	
Hand Action	Secure ball between ankles; jump high in the air	Closer to ball to grab the ball before it touches ground
	Hands low	
	Reach hands out to catch ball before it hits ground	
One-Foot Lift to a Teammate		
Foot Action (Figures 12.6, 12.7)	Put toes under ball, scoop or lift ball to teammate. Foot is used as a scoop. Kick high.	Best surface area. Ball will get up in air.
Partner Action	Catch ball on fly. Big hands.	More surface area to catch the ball
Rule	Ball cannot be caught with hands if ball touches ground	
One-Foot Roll and Lift to Self		
Foot Position (Figure 12.8)	Put sole of foot on top of the ball; roll ball toward yourself quickly	
Foot Action	Put toe of foot under ball	
Foot and Hand Action	Foot is like a springboard; when ball is on toe, flip ball up and catch it with hands	
	Hands low	
Lifting a Rolling Ball to Self		
Foot Action (Figure 12.9)	Put toe of foot downward like a ramp and let ball roll up the foot	Makes the best surface for the ball to roll up
	Keep toe on ground	
Hand Position (Figure 12.10)	Big hands down low by feet	Easier to catch the ball
	Catch ball directly from foot	

Hands low

Squeeze ball between feet

Feet are like pliers

Figure 12.5 Conversion Skills (Two-Legged Lift)

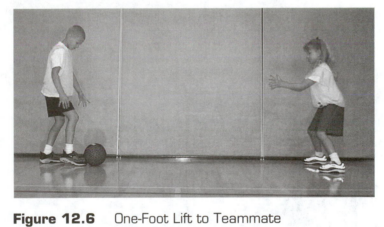

Scoop or lift ball to teammate

Toe under ball

Reach out, big hands

Figure 12.6 One-Foot Lift to Teammate

Kick high

Big hands, catch ball on fly

Figure 12.7 One-Foot Lift to Teammate with Follow-Through

Hands low

Put sole of foot
on top of ball

Figure 12.8   One-Foot Roll and Lift to Self

Foot like a ramp,
roll ball up foot

Figure 12.9   Lift a Rolling Ball to Self

Big hands down
low by feet

Figure 12.10   Lift a Rolling Ball to Self

CATCHING BALL OFF WALL		
Skill	**Cue**	**Why?**
Hand Action (Figure 12.11)	Reach out. Pull ball in.	Teaches students to be aggressive
Eyes	Follow ball flight off wall with eyes	Helps students focus on specific details
Foot Action	Move feet to ball	Positions students correctly to catch ball off an angle off wall
Finger Action	Squeeze the ball	Can hang onto the ball
	Catching the ball before it touches ground makes it an aerial ball	Rule in Quad Ball

Follow ball flight
off wall with eyes

Reach out with hands

Move feet to ball

Figure 12.11   Catching Ball off Wall

KICKING/THROWING BALL AT TENNIS BALL CANS

Skill	Cue	Why?
Kicking Ball at Cans		
Type of Kick	Use either the soccer inside kick or long pass kick	
Eyes	Keep watching the tennis can	Helps focus on target
Throwing Ball at Cans		
Stance	Stand sideways	
Leg Action	Take a step toward target	To be more accurate
Throwing Action	Stretch the arm way back and make an L	More power
Rule	The ball may ricochet off the walls and hit the pins	
Rule	If a defensive player knocks over the offensive team's pin, no point is scored and play resumes	

SOCCER SKILLS

Skill	Cue	Why?
Center Kick		
Rules	The ball must travel forward 1 yard.	
	The kicker may not touch the ball again until another player touches the ball	
	If the ball is kicked in the air, it can be converted into an aerial ball	
Free Kick		
Rules	Is an unchallenged kick in any direction	
	Awarded for an infringement by the opposing side	
	Taken 5 yards away	
Throw-In		
Rules	Take ball straight above head with both hands. Release above head.	
	On release, have thumbs pointing to ground	
	Keep both feet touching ground	

SKILLS FROM OTHER SPORTS		
Skill/Sport	**Skills Used in Quad Ball**	
See Chapter 9: Basketball		
Skills Used	Set shot	
	Right- and left-handed lay-ups without the dribble	
	All of the passing skills	
	Rebounding	
	Pivot	
	Blocking out	
	Defensive stance	
See Chapter 8: Throwing, Catching, Striking, and Kicking		
Skills Used	Throwing, catching, and kicking	
See Chapter 11: Football		
Skills Used	Running in and out plays	
See Chapter 14: Soccer		
Skills Used	Dribble	
	Push-pass	
	Trap	
	Shooting	

Chapter 13

Racket Sports: Tennis and Pickle-Ball

No one can even attempt to describe the stress, intensity, and exhilaration one goes through as they step up to the line to serve for the big point in tennis. No other sport can match the beating the body has received after a 3-hour match played in 105° weather. No other feeling can top the desire to scream a forehand past your opponent after a rally that has made your legs burn. You know it's all up to you. No other game can be as exciting, different, and rewarding for each individual point. No other situation can be as maddening, frustrating, and absolutely glorious as a match of tennis. It gets better every time you step out on the court

Tennis is not only a sport for a lifetime, but also a sport that helps to build character. It teaches you about speed, endurance, agility, anticipation, and quick reaction time. Tennis also tests your mental skills. You learn to control your temper and stay mentally tough to earn those big points that determine who wins the match. To be successful, you must be creative regarding how to combine mental and physical skills. Once you are able to do this, you will learn to construct points. It is very gratifying to put the different shots and strokes together to earn a point. The satisfaction comes when you hit a great shot. You keep coming back to the court for more.

The more you play tennis, the more fun it gets. You can always reach for the next level. This is why we believe tennis to be one of the most fun sports to play.

Pickle-Ball can be played on rainy days or as a separate unit. Use the tennis cues for the forehand, backhand, and volley in Pickle-Ball. Pickle-Ball is played on a badminton (lower the net to tennis net height) or tennis court.

SKILLS LISTED WITH CUES

This chapter presents cues for the following tennis skills: grip, ready position, volley, forehand, backhand, serve, and scoring. Pickle-Ball cues are presented for the following skills: underhand (lob) serve, drive serve, and scoring.

EQUIPMENT TIPS

1. Tennis rackets: Go with the full-size racket (unless a player is really young), because they grow out of them so fast.
2. Lots of tennis balls: at least 10 per student
3. Tennis nets, badminton nets, Pickle-Ball nets, or table tennis nets and tables
4. Pickle-Ball paddles, table tennis rackets
5. Pickle-Ball balls: For better play, order the Pickle-Ball whiffle balls. They have a better bounce.
6. Tennis shoes and comfortable clothing

TEACHING IDEAS

1. If you have equipment for table tennis, introduce this game first, because it isolates the players and prepares them for a court game. Then introduce Pickle-Ball, badminton, and then tennis.
   Sixth grade: Table tennis
   Seventh grade: Pickle-Ball
   Eighth grade: Badminton and tennis
2. When teaching the tennis serve, teach the entire serve. Concentrate on form and not placement. If students are having a tough time, modify the serve. Teach them to "Scratch your back with the racket and throw the ball straight up the chimney."

TEACHING PROGRESSIONS

1. Teach grip and ready position. Move to hitting forehand and backhand volleys, hitting balls with the forehand stroke only, then hitting balls with the backhand stroke only. The next step is to alternate the forehand and the backhand. Then add an underhand serve for Pickle-Ball and a forehand serve for tennis. Play a game with an underhand and forehand serve, using volley forehand and backhand skills. Teach the tennis serve last.
2. Try not to hit in the "donut hole" area of the court. The "donut area" is the center of the court. Why? Because your opponent can stand there, hit the ball back and forth, and move you all over the court. Keep your shots out of the donut hole and hit the donut area. A point to emphasize with the students is that when a ball comes into the donut area on their side of the court, they should recognize it and be aggressive with that shot.

3. When working on positioning, imagine two magnets. One magnet is centered behind the baseline, and the other magnet is at the center of the court, about one to two steps from the net. Have the magnets draw you to one of these two spots on the court. The goal for the receiver is to stay out of "no man's land," which is in the middle of the court. Players can pass you easily by hitting a shot deep into the court.
4. See teaching progressions after each skill.

MINI-GAMES

1. Quarter-Court Games
   * Using volleys, play games inside the service area, where points are scored quickly.
   * The game is started with volley, and the ball is hit directly to the receiver.
   * Players begin to volley the ball back and forth.
   * Whoever has the ball can start the point.
   * You can play games to 7 points and then switch sides.
2. Half-Court Games: Two players play on half of the court. The rules are the same as for a ground stroke game. Play games to 7 points.
3. Ground Stroke Points
   * To put the ball in play, bounce the ball and hit it underhanded anywhere in the opposite court.
   * Singles court lines for singles games and doubles court lines for the doubles.
   * The ball can bounce only once in your court.
   * Whoever has the ball can start the point.
   * Pick a total, such as 11 points, and the first one to reach that score wins. You can play best of three or best of five and rotate with your neighbors.
   * This drill is great for learning to put points together.
5. *Regulation tennis game*: One serve. Only hit a second serve.
6. *Regulation tennis game:* Two serves. You can hit a harder first serve.

Waiting player replaces player missing

Groundstroke

Figure 13.1   Five Misses

7. *Five Misses* (Figure 13.1)

- Four players on a court at a time, with "alternates" at the net post. (There can be just one player at the net post.)
- Players play out a ground stroke point together, and whoever misses goes to the net post.
- One at a time, the alternates replace the misses.
- As soon as a player has five misses, the game is over and a new team is formed.
- You can also do this game with a feeder in one of the posts. The feeder tosses the ball in the court to start play.
- Players rotate around after each point, with alternates at each net post.

FYI

For further information and special help, consult the following organization and source:

Douglas Smith, President
Pickle-Ball, Inc.
801 Northwest 48th Street
Seattle, WA 98107
Phone: (206) 784-4723
Fax: (206) 781-0782

This company provides a free catalog on request. A rule book, a 9-minute videotape of the game of Pickle-Ball, a textbook, and equipment (paddles, ball, nets, standards, and sets) are also available at this address.

Curtis, J. (1985). *Pickle-ball for player and teacher*. Englewood, CO: Morton.

TENNIS—GRIPS		
Skill	**Cue**	**Why?**
Bevel	Top bevel of the racket is #1 Second bevel is #2 Third bevel is #3 Fourth bevel is #4	
Forehand Grip	Shake hands	Puts racket in proper position
(Right-Handed)	Hold the end of the racket	Greater speed with a longer implement and greater reach area to contact the ball
	Index knuckle on third bevel close to fourth bevel (Figure 13.2)	Gives you vertical hitting surface so ball does not go into net or fly long
Backhand Grip	Rotate racket face clockwise Index knuckle on second bevel (Figure 13.3)	The ball flies long if you don't rotate your grip. Remember: "Grip wrong ball long." Gives you vertical hitting surface so ball does not go into net or fly long

Index knuckle on third bevel

Hold the end of racket, shake hands

Figure 13.2   Forehand Grip

Index knuckle on second bevel

Rotate racket face clockwise

Figure 13.3   Right-Hand Backhand Grip

TENNIS—GRIPS

Skill	Cue	Why?
Two-Handed Backhand Grip	Same cues for regular backhand	Quick reaction time
(Right-Handed)	Keep left hand up to anticipate hitting a backhand	More power with two hands
	Grip left hand above right hand on racket	Proper racket position
	Left index knuckle on third bevel	
Right-Handed Players	Right-handed players rotate bevels in a clockwise direction	
Left-Handed Players	Left-handed players rotate bevels in a counterclockwise direction	

TENNIS—VOLLEYS

Skill	Cues	Why?
Forehand Volley	Index knuckle on second bevel for both forehand and backhand	No time to change for quicker reaction time to ball
	Pivot, step, and punch	Power
	Firm wrist, firm grip (Figure 13.4)	Prevent the racket from coming out of hand, especially if the ball is hit hard into the racket
	Hand below ball; racket and wrist form L. Don't let racket head drop.	Firm contact when you hit the ball. Better control and accuracy.
	Racket stays in front of front shoulder. Put string attached to racquet head and nose.	Keeps you aggressive at the net. Better accuracy of your shot.
	Keep racket in peripheral vision	Faster reaction time
	Be aggressive. In this shot, go get the ball. Don't wait for the ball to come to you.	Places the opponent on the defensive
	Bend at the knees and keep the back vertical	

TENNIS—VOLLEYS

Skill	Cues	Why?
Backhand Volley	Same as backhand cues, just hitting on backhand side Index knuckle on second bevel (Figure 13.5)	

Firm wrist and grip

Hand below ball

Pivot, step, and punch

Figure 13.4   Forehand Volley

Racket stays in front of shoulder

Pivot, step, and punch

Figure 13.5   Backhand Volley

TENNIS—FOREHAND STROKE (RIGHT HAND)		
Skill	**Cues**	**Why**
Grip	Index knuckle on third bevel close to fourth bevel	The ball does not go high, and you can get under the ball
Footwork	Pivot and step	Good position for ball contact
Stroke Action [Figure 13.6]	Racket back early/closed face	Good preparation. Ball won't fly high and out of bounds.

TENNIS—FOREHAND STROKE (RIGHT HAND)

Skill	Cues	Why
Contact Point [Figure 13.7]	Contact point: racket is in vertical plane	Accuracy
	Hit ball even with front hip	Accuracy
Finish and Follow-Through [Figure 13.8]	Swing racket from low to high and finish on edge	
	Point elbow toward the opponent when done	To get good topspin. Ball won't go out of bounds.
	Kiss your bicep	The friction created with "over the ball motion" will give more powerful topspin
Ball Goes into Net	Bend knees and get low	Ball will not go into net if you get low and bend your knees

Teaching Progression

1. Always check grip first.
2. To practice the grip, have students bounce the ball with their rackets, using the appropriate grip. They can bounce the ball up or down and count how many times they do it.
3. Have players stand 1 to 2 feet away from the tennis fence. Start with the racket head back and in the closed position; swing the racket to contact point. Make sure the racket is vertical. On the follow-through, the racket goes over the opposite shoulder and the elbow points toward the opposite court. Swing from low to high and finish "kissing the bicep." Step 5 feet away from the fence, drop the ball, and hit into the fence.
4. When the students' strokes are done with control, move to the court. Drop-hit a ball over the net. Give them a target to aim for. For example, hit down the alley.
5. Next, teach the students how to toss to a partner. One partner tosses a ball underhanded so that it bounces 5 to 8 feet in front of the partner. They should toss a ball back and forth until they have achieved good accuracy. The ball should bounce at least waist-high.

Racket back
early, closed face

Pivot and step

Figure 13.6   Racket Back Early

Racket in
vertical plane

Figure 13.7   Contact Point (Forehand)

6. When ready, the students toss the ball to their partners. The tosser stands off to the side of the net and tosses balls to the partner, who is standing at the service line ready to stroke the ball (Figure 13.9).

7. The tosser stands on one side of the net and tosses balls to his partner, who is standing on the baseline ready to stroke the ball. Encourage the students that it doesn't matter where the ball lands, but stress the importance of good form on their stroke. When they have some accuracy, allow them to hit forehands back and forth with their partners.

Swing racket from
low to high and finish
on edge

Figure 13.8   Forehand Follow-Through

Tosser stands off
to side of net and
tosses the ball to
hitter

Hitter strokes ball
from service line

Figure 13.9   Partner Forehand Drill

TENNIS–BACKHAND STROKE (RIGHT HAND)

Skill	Cues	Why?
Grip	Left hand up early, grab racket	Reaction time
	Right-hand index knuckle to second bevel	Accuracy for shot
Footwork	Pivot and step	To get in good position to hit the ball
Stroke Action	Bend at knees, back vertical	Better shot accuracy
	Racket back early, face closed low by your shoelaces (Figure 13.10)	Better power, better accuracy
Contact Point	Contact point racket is vertical and off the front hip (Figure 13.11)	So ball will land in court
Finish	Follow through from low to high and racket finishes over opposite shoulder—"Kiss your biceps" (Figure 13.12)	To achieve topspin

Bend knees

Racket back early, face closed

Figure 13.10 Racket Back Early (Two-Hand Backhand)

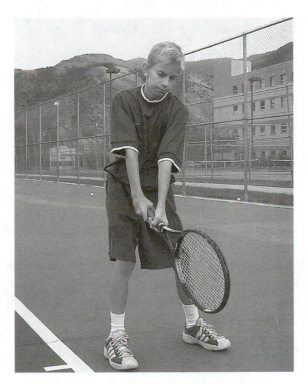

Racket and contact point vertical

Figure 13.11   Contact Point (Two-Hand Backhand)

Racket finishes over opposite shoulder

Follow through from low to high

Figure 13.12   Backhand Follow-Through

Teaching Progression for Backhand

1. Demonstrate the backhand grip. Line students along the fence and have them shadow-swing from low to high following the cues.
2. One partner drop-feeds the ball to the other partner. Hit the ball into the fence.
3. When they feel comfortable with the stroke, line students on the baselines and have partners feed. Give them a target at which to hit the ball in the court (e.g., down the line or cross-court).
4. When the students are ready, one student stands off to the side of the net and tosses balls to the partner, who is standing at the service line, ready to stroke the ball (Figure 13.13).
5. Have one partner feed ball into the court from the other side of the net.
6. Rally backhand to backhand.
7. One partner tosses the ball to alternating sides of the other partner: forehand, backhand, forehand, backhand, and so on. This drill causes players to change grips, and move feet to the ball, and helps them determine how to hit backhands in a gamelike situation.
8. Teach a ground stroke game. It incorporates all the skills they have learned and gives them gamelike practice with lots of repetitions.

Tosser stands off to side of net and tosses ball to hitter

Hitter strokes ball from service line

Figure 13.13 Partner Backhand Drill

TENNIS—SERVE (RIGHT HAND)

Skill	Cue	Why?
Grip	Right hand index knuckle on #2 bevel	Accuracy and control
Foot Placement	Point left foot toward right net post or, if left-handed, right foot toward left net post	This allows good shoulder rotation and power
	Back foot in comfortable position	Stability and balance
Toss	Hold ball in fingerpads	Control of ball
	Hold ball down by leg	Control and accuracy of toss
	Gently toss ball high	Timing for serve
	Keep arm straight all the way up	Accuracy of toss
	Hold arm up until ball contacts racket	You will "feel" the ball better
Stroking Action	Hit high and in front of you	Power and good contact point. Racket head speed is the fastest up there.
	Racket motion is just like throwing a ball	Creates a powerful serve
Follow-Through	Arm action comes across the body	Completes the motion of your serve and power isn't lost
	The shoulder of the arm that hit the serve ends up where the other shoulder was	The movement naturally provides more power, as body weight goes into serve

Teaching Progression

1. Teach the ball toss first. Place the racket on the ground at a 30-degree angle, and place foot at the end of the handle. Toss the ball up and try to hit the strings of the racket.
2. Have students throw a ball into the service box. If they can *throw* it into the box, they can *serve* it into the box
3. Teach the entire serve.
4. If students have difficulty with the serve, have them start the serve with the racket up behind the head (Figure 13.14)
5. Allow beginners to serve up close, and then move back to the baseline when they are ready.

Start serve with racket behind head

Figure 13.14   Serve Progression

TENNIS—SCORING		
Skills	**Cues**	**Why?**
Singles/Doubles	Love (0), 15, 30, 40, game 15–0 = 15–love 0–15 = love–15 30–30 = 30 all 40–40 = deuce	
Deuce	Ad in: service advantage Ad out: opponent's advantage The player who wins 2 points in a row wins the game	This makes it possible for someone to come back and win at any time
Set	Change sides on odd-numbered games: 1, 3, 5, 7 Win six games and win by two games.	If you lose the first set, you can still have a chance to win
Women's Match (Pro Tennis)	Win two out of three sets	
Men's Match (Pro Tennis)	Win three out of five sets	

PICKLE-BALL—SERVES

Skill	Cue	Why?
Lob Serve	One foot in front of baseline; other foot in back of baseline	Serving rule
		Ball will go high
	Drop the ball, then swing the paddle underhand	
	Like pitching horseshoes	
Drive Serve	Follow through straight up to touch face with biceps	Serving rule
	Finish like Statue of Liberty	It's a flatter serve, like the forehand stroke in tennis. This allows ball to go close to net.
	One foot in front of baseline; other foot in back of baseline	
	Ball held waist-high and out in front	
	Paddle is held behind you waist-high, wrist in locked position	
	Drop the ball, then swing	
	Paddle finishes on edge	
	Swing low to high	

PICKLE-BALL—SCORING

Skill	Cue	Why?
Singles	Can only score a point when serving	
	When score is zero or even, serve in right court	
	When score is odd number, serve in left court	
Doubles (for more information, see FYI page 154)	Ball must bounce once in receiver's court as well as once in server's court on the return	
	Remember bounce–bounce	
	Play to 11 points, win by 2	

Chapter 14

Soccer

Soccer is a game that everyone can play, a game that keeps you fit and challenges you to the max. Soccer has been around for centuries and is played the world over. It has been termed the *Sport of the World,* and rightly so, because it is played in every country of the world. In most countries, it is more commonly known as *football,* and here in the United States it is known as *soccer.* What makes it so exciting is the challenge of a whole team trying to score. Soccer is a simple game, one that your elementary and middle school students will enjoy.

SKILLS LISTED WITH CUES

The following soccer skills are included in this chapter: ball control and ball control drills; the dribble and dribbling drills; passing and two-player passing; chipping and two- to three-player chipping drills; the long pass and two-player drills; trapping and trapping drills; kicking and shooting drills; heading; goalkeeping; and defense and offense.

EQUIPMENT TIPS

The first thing you need to consider is proper equipment.

1. A size 4-inch soccer ball is appropriate for 8- to 12-year-olds. A 12-inch ball is appropriate for 12 years and older. This size ball is designed in relationship to the size of the students. Other small balls are also appropriate, such as Nerf or rubber playground balls.
2. One ball for every two to four students is recommended to practice skills. The students can work in small groups, with no standing in line waiting for a turn. This maximizes student involvement.
3. Students should wear comfortable clothes that are appropriate for hot weather.

4. Comfortable shoes (no sandals): Cleats are not needed at this level of play. Decide whether cleated shoes will be allowed in class. Be aware that some toes may get stepped on. However, cleated shoes *are* recommended for recreational soccer teams.

5. Shin guards are important in preventing injury to the anterior compartment of the shin (very little room for tissue and blood). It is recommended that all students have a pair, especially for games.

6. The field of play can be an actual soccer field or an open, grassy area at the school or a nearby park.

7. Use cones to outline the field. Flags can be substituted for goals. Half cones are great to use in drills. You can make a set of goals 3 feet high by 3 feet wide out of PVC pipe.

8. Use colored vests to divide students into teams.

TEACHING IDEAS

1. A warm-up should be included with every class practice. A proper warm-up includes moderate physical activity, such as jogging or a game of keep-away with the soccer ball. This, along with proper stretching, decreases the likelihood of injury.
   - Warm-up
   - Elevation of heart rate
   - Breaking a sweat is important
   - Ideas for warm-ups: running and dynamic stretching (see Chapters 6 and 7).

2. Safety Concerns
   - Emphasize the importance of playing with control and being aware of others' personal space. Use mini-games to reduce the number of players in a game situation.
   - Be prepared for accidents. Have a first-aid kit available and a first-aid plan.
   - Have plenty of water available during the activity, especially on a hot day.
   - Avoid playing during the heat of the day when possible.
   - Ensure no wearing of jewelry, shirts tucked in, and proper clothing for weather conditions.
   - Have proper warm-up and cool-down periods to prevent possible muscle injuries.
   - Remember to teach to the specific age level. Don't demand too much.

TEACHING PROGRESSION

See the skills section for gamelike drills.

MINI-GAMES

1. Play games of 3 on 3, 4 on 4, and 5 on 5.
2. Scoring options in these games: ball goes over endline, 1 point; ball goes through two cones, 1 point.

FYI

For further information and special help, consult the following organizations:

American Youth Soccer Organization (AYSO)
5403 West 138th Street
Hawthorne, CA 90250
Phone: (310) 643-6455
Fax: (310) 643-5310
http://www.ayso.org

National Soccer Coaches Association of America (NSCAA)
6700 Squibb Road, Suite 215
Mission, KS 66202
Phone: (800) 458-0678
Fax: (913) 362-3439
http://www.nscaa.com/

United States Soccer Federation (USSF)
1801-1811 South Prairie Avenue
Chicago, IL 60616
Phone: (312) 808-1300
Fax: (312) 808-1301
http://www.us-soccer.com

US Youth Soccer Association
899 Presidential Drive, Suite 117
Richardson, TX 75081
Phone: 1-800-4SOCCER
http://www.usysa.org/

FIFA Fédération Internationale de Football Association
FIFA House, 11 Hitzigweg, 8030 Zurich, Switzerland
FIFA, P.O. Box 85, 8030 Zurich, Switzerland
Phone: +41-1/384 9595
Fax: +41-1/384 9696
http://www.fifa.com

BALL CONTROL/BALL CONTROL DRILLS

Skill	Cue	Why?
Ball Control		
Knowing Ball	Kicking the ball	To get familiar with the ball and how it works
Kicking Top of Ball	Ball goes down (ball stays low)	Keeps ball low and in control
Kicking Middle of Ball	Ball goes straight	
Kicking Bottom of Ball (Figure 14.1)	Ball goes up (like a pop-up in softball)	For chipping and defensive clears
Kicking Left Side of Ball	Ball goes right	
Kicking Right Side of Ball	Ball goes left	
Ball Control Drills		
Juggling Ball	Try to keep the ball in the air, using the feet, as long as you can. Your goal would be 2 balls, then 3, then 4. If players can do between 5 and 10, they have good ball control.	This increases ball touches, familiarity with the ball, thus increasing ball control skills
Experimenting with Ball (Partner Drill)	Players strike the ball on the five surfaces listed in column 1.	Again, just getting familiar with all the different surfaces

Kick bottom of ball

Ball goes up like pop-up in softball

Figure 14.1   Ball Control

DRIBBLE/DRIBBLE DRILLS

Skill	Cue	Why?
Dribble Technique *Dribble Ball with Different Surfaces of Foot* (Figure 14.2)	Caress ball in stride Inside, outside, sole, or laces	If you push the ball too far ahead, a defender can easily steal it away
	Close control/Keep ball close	Keeps ball close and under control, which makes it much more difficult for the defender to gain possession
	Push firmly	
	Head up, pull chin back	
	Arms out, with elbows bent for balance	
Action of Dribble	Depending on the situation, change pace and direction	
Dribble Drills *Six or Seven Cones for Each Small Group*	Dribble through cones (weave through cones)	Learn how to keep control of the ball while dribbling
	Cones help players control the ball. The goal is for the player to stay in close proximity to the cones.	
	Races	

Caress ball
during stide

Keep ball close

Push ball firmly

Figure 14.2   Dribble

PASSING/PASSING DRILLS

Skills	Cue	Why?
Passing		
Push Pass	Pendulum swing with the foot (like on a grandfather's clock)	For easy, quick passes to a teammate
Foot Position	Ankle firm	
Inside	Strike ball with instep of foot	
Outside	Strike ball with outside of foot	
Laces	Strike ball with laces, not the toe	Don't toe ball, because there is no accuracy
Striking the Ball Action	Knee over ball	To have more control and the ball won't go flying up in the air
Two-Player Passing Drills		
5- to 10-Yard Passes	Pass back and forth to partner, using different surfaces of foot	Gain familiarity with the technique of the push pass
	Kicking with right and left foot gives you an edge over the average player, who can't pass with both feet	
Passing Accuracy	Player 1 stands with legs shoulder-width apart and player 2 tries to pass the ball through partner's legs. Switch positions.	Gain accuracy with the push pass

CHIPPING/CHIPPING DRILLS

Skill	Cue	Why?
Chipping the Ball		
Eyes	Focus on the bottom part of the ball	Clears the ball out of the defense, or for a pass over the opposing team to one of your teammates
Approach	Approach the ball straight on	
Action	It's a quick, hard stab under the ball (like a shovel)	
	Bring your knee toward your chest	
Two-Player Chipping Drill		
10 to 20 Yards Apart	Practice chipping to each other	
Accuracy		
In pairs, make a box 5 to 10 feet square, with cones for each partner. The distance from each box is variable.	Two players are standing in their own grid. Have them chip to their partner.	
Three-Player Chipping Drill	Player 1 passes the ball to player 2, who passes ball to player 3, and player 3 tries to chip the ball over player 2 to player 1	
	Rotate players in each position: Each player goes to the position spot they passed to. 1 goes to 2's spot, 2 goes to 3's spot, and 3 goes to 1's spot. Repeat.	

LONG PASS/LONG PASS DRILLS

Skill	Cue	Why?
Long Pass		Used for crosses and shooting
Ankle	Ankles firm (no floppy feet)	Stronger, more controlled pass
	Take a slightly angled approach	
Nonkicking Foot	Place it next to the ball	Helps create greater velocity in kicking foot
	Toe is pointing at target, so ball will go to target	
Kicking Foot	Strike the ball with laces and inside of foot	More surface is on the ball, better control
Used for Corner Kicks and Clears	Follow through with the foot pointed and leg toward the target	
	Strike the ball where the ball touches the grass. Keep your ankle locked when striking. Your leg kicks up and into the ball with a good follow-through.	
Two-Player Drills		
At Least 20 Yards Apart	Player 1 passes to player 2. Pass back and forth. Have players take a step backward each time they do a successful pass at that distance.	

TRAPPING/TRAPPING DRILLS

Skill	Cue	Why?
Trapping		To gain quick possession of an uncontrolled ball
Trap	Absorb ball and soften the hit by moving your body away slowly	Controls the ball, brings it right to your feet
Different Surfaces	Cushion the ball—stop the ball as if catching an egg	

TRAPPING/TRAPPING DRILLS

Skill	Cue	Why?
Trapping (*cont'd*)		
Foot	Trap ball with soft feet	
Thigh (Figure 14.3)	Trap ball with upper front of thigh	
Chest (Figure 14.4)	Trap ball with breastbone	
Head	Trap ball with forehead	
Receiving the Pass	Present the trapping surface to the ball. Take the pace off the ball by withdrawing the body part as soon as the ball is received.	
Trapping Drills		
Each Player Has a Ball	Have the player throw the ball up in the air, and practice using the different surfaces to trap the ball	Helps player practice the skills of trapping

Present trapping surface to ball

Cushion ball as if catching an egg

Trap ball with upper part of thigh

Figure 14.3   Thigh Trap

Present trapping surface to ball

Trap ball with breakbone

Soften the hit by moving your body away slowly

Figure 14.4   Chest Trap

KICKING/SHOOTING AND KICKING/SHOOTING DRILLS

Skill	Cue	Why?
The Kick		
A striking action executed with the feet (e.g., the long pass kick, corner kick, goal kicks)	Body is stationary and leg is straight, with little flex at the knee. There is minimal movement of the arms and the trunk. Concentrate on the ball. Hold arms out for balance.	
The Shot	Like firing a cannonball	
Leg	Pull back the kicking leg; have it pointing at the target	
Nonkicking Foot	Place the nonkicking foot alongside the ball, toes pointing at the target	Ball goes where the toes point
Kicking Foot	After shooting, follow through. After the follow-through, land on the kicking foot (not the nonkicking foot).	Puts more power and control in the stroke
Ankle (of Kicking Foot)	Ankle is firm, toes are pointing down	
Head	Keep head down and chest over the ball to keep the ball low	
Kicking/Shooting Drills		
Each player has a ball, facing the goal	Each player can practice shooting on the goal (there is no need for a goalie at this time). Balls shouldn't be retrieved until all the balls are shot, to prevent injuries.	

HEADING

Skills	Cue	Why?
Head	Strike ball with top of forehead (where the hairline meets the forehead)	It doesn't hurt when heading on the hairline. More control.
Eyes	Keep eyes open—watch the ball meet your forehead	
Upper Body	Draw upper body back (pull shoulders back)	It will provide more power in the header
Chin	Pull chin in	
Follow-Through	You strike the ball—do not let the ball hit you	No power in the header if you let it hit you
Torso	Snap the upper body forward to meet the ball. (Whip the body through the ball.)	Most of the power comes from here
Offensive Header	Head downward toward goal	Use offensive header for passing and shooting
Defensive Header	Head upward	Used to clear the danger area

THROW-INS

Skill	Cue	Why?
Throw-Ins	When the ball crosses the touchline into out-of-bounds, it is thrown back onto the field (which is the only time a field player may touch the ball with the hands). Stand where the ball crossed the line and throw from behind the head (USSF rules).	
The Throw (Figures 14.5 and 14.6)	Face the field	
	Use both hands	
	Start behind the head, and throw over the head (follow through with both hands)	
	Keep both feet behind the touchline. Both feet have to stay on the ground.	
	Arms throw outward	

Start from behind head
and throw over the head

Keep feet behind
touch line

Figure 14.5   Soccer Throw-In (Hand/Arm
Position, Side View)

Both feet have to
stay on the ground

Figure 14.6   Soccer Throw-In (Hand/Arm
Position, Front View)

THROW-INS		
Skill	**Cue**	**Why?**
Follow-Through [Figure 14.7]	Body snaps through the throw	More power in the throw
Short and Close Throw	Snap (arms snap down, hands and palms down)	
High and Low Throw	Snap up! Throw up and over.	

Arms throw outwards

Body snaps through the throw

Follow through with both hands

Figure 14.7   Soccer Throw-In (Follow-Through)

GOALKEEPING

Skill	Cue	Why?
Receiving Low Balls	Goalie calls for the ball	
	Scoop into body with hands outstretched, fingers spread. Wrap it up.	
Hand Positions for Catching in Air	Big hands!	
	The "M"—palms up, pinkies together. Used to receive low balls.	
	"Hershey Kiss" or "triangle." Palms out, pointer fingers touching, and thumbs create a "Hershey Kiss" or triangle.	So ball will not slip through fingers
Punching	Clear the ball away from the goal, using a flat surface on the hand.	
	Used for high balls hit over the top of the goal. Used when diving to hit the ball away from the goal.	

GOALKEEPING

Skill	Cue	Why?
Diving (Figures 14.8 and 14.9)	Lunge and cover lots of area with body	
	When diving, land on the outer of the thigh, hip, and side of the upper body. Don't land on the knees.	
	Reach out with hands	
	Catch the ball and pull it in	
Distributing Ball	There are different ways to distribute the ball back to the field players: Punting Rolling Throwing (see Chapter 8) Javelin throw	

Big hands

Lunge and cover lots of area

Figure 14.8   Goalie Dive

Land on outer thigh, hip, and side of body

Reach out with hands, catch ball, and pull in

Figure 14.9   Goalie Dive Landing

DEFENSE

Skill	Cue	Why?
Objectives	Regain possession Deny penetration Slow down attack Stop shots	
Stance	Bend knees slightly, bend elbows (ready for action), eyes on the ball and the opponent	
Tips	Keep goalside of your opponent	
	Be first to the ball	
	Defend the ball, not the player	

OFFENSE

Skill	Cue	Why?
Dribbling	Keep head up; look for a pass	
	Body forward and erect	
Off the Ball	Get goalside of the opponent	
	Penetrate the defense	
	Move into empty space, always creating chances	

Chapter 15

Softball, Slow-Pitch

How many of you have memories of playing softball in the summer? Imagine the thrill your students will have when they can throw, catch, and strike a softball for the first time. If your students can hone these skills, they will have the necessary tools to play softball for a lifetime. Lifetime participation may include playing on a city recreation team or at family reunions and outings, or playing catch in the back yard with a friend. It's definitely an American pastime, and students need to be familiar with the skills and rules.

SKILLS LISTED WITH CUES

The skills presented in this chapter include throwing, catching, baserunning, underhand slow pitch, batting, catcher position, infield ground balls, and outfield skills.

EQUIPMENT TIPS

1. Rubber softballs, soft softballs, regulation softballs, 6-inch playground balls (Figure 15.1)
2. Aluminum bats
3. Gloves that properly fit hand, if available
4. Rubber bases
5. Catcher's equipment
6. Batting helmets

Regulation   Rubber   Soft

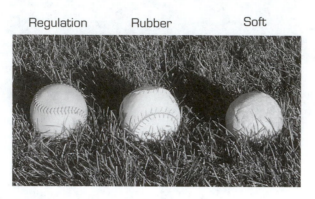

Figure 15.1   Ball Textures

EQUIPMENT TIPS FOR YOUNGER STUDENTS

1. Younger students should play with a whiffle ball or a soft softball.
2. A plastic bat
3. Suspended rope with an attached ball at the end for batting practice. For younger grades, see Pangrazi (2001) and Graham, Holt/Hale, and Parker (2001) for softball activities.
4. Use batting tees to practice hitting the ball.

TEACHING IDEAS

1. Make sure students know how to perform the fundamental skills of throwing, catching, fielding, and running the bases before you play mini-games.
2. *Always* emphasize batting safety. A batter should wear a helmet, either while hitting or when on deck. Students and teachers need to stay behind the backstop or in the dugout.
3. Maximize participation with games such as Softball Throwbee and Throw It around the Horn.
4. Softball has a complex set of rules and skills. Teachers need to be sensitive to the rate at which each student learns the skill.

TEACHING PROGRESSIONS

1. Partner throwing and catching
2. Throw ground and fly balls to partner
3. *Throw It around the Horn* (infield practice) (Figure 15.2)
   - The goal is to have the student aim the ball at the player's chest. This teaches the students to throw and aim for a specific target.
   - Catcher throws to first, first throws to shortstop, shortstop throws to second, second throws to third, third throws back to pitcher, and the pitcher practices the pitch. Repeat. Rotate positions after a set number of repetitions.

Aim ball at
player's chest

Infield
throwing drill

Figure 15.2   Throw It around the Horn

- You can choose different sequences for throwing around the horn.
- Lots of practice time
4. Play lots of mini-games to maximize participation and minimize wait time

MINI-GAMES

1. Softball Throwbee (Figure 15.3) (see Chapter 8)
   - Play with a rubber softball or soft softball
   - The batter throws the ball anywhere in the field. Play with regulation softball rules.
   - This game teaches softball skills, and its rules eliminate the danger of players getting hit with a bat.
2. Ryan's Ball (developed by Janet Ryan at Springcreek Middle School, Providence, Utah)
   - A modified game to practice batting skills
   - Played with a 6-inch playground ball
   - Uses the skills of running, throwing, catching, and batting
   - No gloves or mitts needed

Batter throws ball
anywhere on field

Play regulation
softball rules

Figure 15.3   Throwbee

- Many opportunities to respond to the basic skills covered throughout the game
- Teams of seven students to maximize gamelike practice
- The field team has a catcher, first base, second base, third base, shortstop, and two outfielders. We recommend having the pitcher be from the hitting team.
- Keep the rules as close to those of softball as possible.
- You need to maximize opportunities to respond by decreasing the number of balls "pitched" to three.
- Decrease the number of outs to two.
- If there are two games, with four teams, try to have another adult supervise the batting area.

MODIFIED SOFTBALL GAMES

- Once the students acquire the concepts and skills of softball, introduce the game of softball, using a soft softball, and introduce gloves. It is important that the students have a maximum number of opportunities to respond, while having fun, and being safe when up to bat.
- Only three pitches are allowed.
- A teacher or a skilled student pitches the ball.
- Everybody bats.
- Keep the teams as small as possible.
- You may need additional adults supervising the batting area, depending on the age of the class members.

FYI

For further information, consult the following books:

Pangrazi, R. (2001). *Dynamic physical education for elementary school children* (13th ed.). Boston: Allyn and Bacon.

Graham, G., Holt/Hale, S. A., & Parker, M. (2001). *Children moving.* Mountain View, CA: Mayfield.

THROWING

Skill	Cue	Why?
Right-Handed		
Stance	Stand sideways	More power; ball will go farther using entire body. Less strain on the arm, less chance of injury.
Leg Action	Take a long step toward the target	More power; ball will go farther. Helps direct the ball to the target.
Arm Action	Stretch the arm down; brush the shorts	
Elbow Action	Stretch the arm way back and make an L	More power and direction on the ball
Release Point	Release at 2:00 position	Ball does not go too low or high. Better accuracy.
Follow-Through	Turn palm out on follow-through	More speed on the ball. Better accuracy.
Left-Handed	Same as above	
	Release at 10:00 position	

Skill Progression

Avoid speed and distance contests when first teaching how to throw a ball. Learning the fundamentals comes first, and decreases the chance of students' arms getting injured.

CATCHING

Skill	Cue	Why?
Catching without a Glove		
Hand Position	Spread fingers—Big Hands	Covers more surface area on the ball
Arm Action	Reach out arms and hands; bring ball into stomach	The ball won't hit the student
		Allows a player to see the ball all the way into the glove
Finger Action	Quiet, soft hands when you catch ball	More absorption of the ball and a smoother catch
Focus Point	Eyes keep watching ball all the way into body. Head down.	Students have tendency to turn head and be afraid of ball
Catching above Waist		
Hand Position	Reach out, hands in front of you	Most effective surface area for hands. Hands are big and in best position to catch ball.
	Hands up, thumbs up, and make wide fingers	
	Hands up; move to the ball	
Catching below Waist	Pinkies up and make wide fingers	Most effective surface area for hands. Hands are big and in best position to catch ball.
Catching with a Glove	Hold the nonglove hand up with the glove hand when catching a ball	
	Open the glove wide	Bigger surface area to catch the ball
	Watch the ball all the way into the glove	
	When you feel the ball hit the glove, close it	If you squeeze tight, the ball will not drop out
	Have nonglove hand close to the glove to help keep the ball in and be ready to make the throw	If the ball slips out of the glove, the other hand can help the ball stay in, plus you are ready to make a throw

INFIELD GROUND BALL

Skill	Cue	Why?
Stance (Figure 15.4)	Bend knees and have glove open in front of you, with fingers of glove touching ground	Balance, stability
	Make a triangle with glove and feet	Ball won't go through legs
Moving to the Ball	Watch the ball off the bat	Quickens reaction time to the ball and increases range
	When ground ball is hit, beat the ball to the spot	
	Get your body in front of the ball by shuffling your feet	Better control of the ball. The ball won't get past you.
	Keep glove wide open	More surface area for the ball to go into
Eyes	Watch the ball all the way into the glove	Eyes focusing on ball offers better chance to catch it
Catching Action	Close the glove when the ball hits it	Ball will stay in glove
Nonglove Action	Keep your free hand next to the glove to help the ball stay in and to be ready to throw	Better chance for the ball to stay in the glove. If the ball slips out of the glove, the free hand is there to help it back in.
	Always catch the ball with two hands	The free hand is close to the ball for a faster throw. Helps keep ball in glove.

Watch ball all the way into glove

Make a triangle with glove and feet

Keep glove in front and on the ground

Figure 15.4   Infield Ground Ball

FLY BALL SKILLS

Skill	Cue	Why?
Fly Ball		
Eyes	Watch the ball off the bat	See what direction the ball is going
Moving to the Ball (Figure 15.5)	Run to get underneath the ball hit in the air. Beat the ball to the spot.	Ball won't go over your head Easier to run forward, then backwards. First step is always back.
	Set your glove above your head. Open the glove wide.	More surface area for the ball to land
	Watch the ball all the way into the glove	
Glove Action	Close the glove as soon as the ball hits it. Use both hands.	Ball won't come out
Free Hand	Keep your free hand next to the glove to help the ball stay in and to be ready to throw	The free hand is close to the ball for a faster throw

Watch the ball all the way into the glove

Beat the ball to the spot

Get your glove above your head and open the glove wide

Figure 15.5　Fly Ball

UNDERHAND PITCH

Skill	Cue	Why?
Technique (Figure 15.6)	Start with the ball in glove	
	Make a straight arm, swing arm backwards to shoulder level, bend knees	
	Like a pendulum swing ball forward	More power and accuracy with ball
	Step forward with opposite leg	Power to get ball up in the air
	Swing arm forward	
	Release the ball after the ball passes the hip and before the arm is parallel to shoulder	Arc and speed are created on the ball to get the ball over the plate

Swing the arm
straight back

Pendulum swing ball
forward

Step forward
with opposite
leg, bend knees

Figure 15.6   Underhand Pitch

BATTING

Skill	Cue	Why?
Stance (Figure 15.7)	Stand parallel to the side of plate. Feet shoulder-width apart.	Balance and control
Bat Position	Hold bat with fists touching each other about 1 inch above end of handle of bat	Able to snap wrist and gain power
	Middle knuckles lined up	Able to swing bat level

Middle knuckles lined up

Stand sideways with feet shoulder width apart

Figure 15.7   Batting Stance

BATTING		
Skill	**Cue**	**Why?**
Batting Action	Back elbow up. Make an upside-down V	
	Form V with arms and catch ball on way down	
	Step forward with front leg, while rotating hips	Stepping into the ball generates more power and distance on the ball
	Swing shoulder to shoulder	If your swing is level, you will know where to move the bat head to hit the ball
	If ball is in strike zone, step forward with front foot, swing bat level, and watch ball hit bat	*Always* watch the ball hit the bat. If you take your eyes off the ball, you have less chance of hitting the ball.
	Roll both wrists over on follow-through	More distance to the ball

THE CATCHER

Skill	Cue	Why?
Protective Equipment	Facemask, shin guards, chest protector mandatory	Protects you from foul balls, etc.
Stance	Start in squatting position Weight on inside of feet	A catcher should never be behind the batter unless wearing all the protective gear, especially in a squatting position
Glove Position	Hold glove with pinkie turned up in strike zone Open glove wide	Catch ball in strike zone Gives the pitcher a good target. Catcher is more mobile and balanced.
High Pitch	Spring up if pitch is high	More surface area for the ball to be caught. Less likely to drop the ball.
Low Pitch	If ball is low or in the dirt, turn wrist over, hold glove like a scoop Throw ball back to pitcher	Reaction time faster to catch the ball Able to scoop ball off ground faster and play ball out of dirt

BASERUNNING

Skill	Cues	Why?
Baserunning	As soon as you hit the ball, run to first base Sprint hard all the way through first base	
Rule to First Base	You can overrun first, but after you touch first base, you have to turnout and run out of bounds	The batter should run the minute the ball hits the bat, even if the ball might be going foul

BASERUNNING

Skill	Cues	Why?
Running First Base to Home (Figure 15.8)	While running toward the bases, take an angle so you can touch the inside corner of each base	You increase your running time and distance by not taking a wide angle. You decrease your chance of tripping over a base.
	Spring hard between bases	Also, keeps the shoulder and momentum toward the field
	Be aware of what base you are on and whether there is a runner on the base in front of you or behind you	If there is a runner behind you and the ball is hit, you must run to the next base before the infielder gets there, or it is called a force-out.

Touch inside corner of each base

Sprint hard between bases

Figure 15.8   Baserunning

Chapter 16

Track and Field

Track and field, the world's first sport, is an event that allows individual growth and competition. Children develop a great sense of individuality and an understanding of their body's capabilities. Because of the vast number of events, such as sprinting, hurdling, jumping, and throwing, children can recognize the events at which they are best and enjoy the most. Track and field allows individuals to shine when they may not in other sports because of their size, abilities, and coordination.

SKILLS LISTED WITH CUES

This chapter presents cues for the following track and field events: block starts, starts, hurdles, standing long jump, running long jump, triple jump, and relay. See Chapter 6 for dynamic stretches and core exercises and Chapter 7 for sprinting drills.

EQUIPMENT TIPS

1. Stop watches
2. Adjustable hurdles, elementary hurdles, or orange cones with bars on them
3. Running shoes
4. Starting blocks
5. Batons
6. Grass or tumbling mats for the jumps

TEACHING IDEAS

1. Use toilet paper for the finish line. Race two or three students, who have about the same times, for a 40- or 50-yard dash. If you have lane lines, work on staying in between the lane lines.
2. On the triple jump, have students try to hop, step, then hop, step, jump, and then have them run, hop, step, and jump. Have them land on the grass outside. Practice this skill so that all students are jumping at the same time on the grass. Save the jumping pit for when their skills are more developed. Don't do more than six to 10 jumps per day.

TEACHING PROGRESSIONS

1. The warm-up should be easy jogging, dynamic stretches, and core exercises (see Chapter 6).
2. *Always* perform the four sprinting drills and acceleration drills found in Chapter 7.
3. For hurdles, start with eight steps to the first hurdle. Practice the block start, running eight steps and going over only one hurdle.

MINI-GAMES

1. Three-Person Chase: Have the students line up in sets of three. On your command, bring them through the first two start commands: "Runners on your mark," "set." The middle student will then come out of her blocks at her discretion. The other two students will then chase the middle runner. Rotate until all students have been in the middle position.
2. Jump for distance individually or work in cooperative groups.
3. Set up 12- to 24-inch collapsible hurdles, eight steps apart. Students take turns running over the hurdles, practicing rhythm and proper form.
4. Play games such as Ultimate Frisbee, soccer, basketball, and so on, to work on sprinting skills.

FYI

Jamie Hall/Bennion
USA Track and Field Level 2 Coach
Mountain Crest Track and Field Head Coach, Hyrum, Utah
Rocky Mountain Elite Track and Field Coach, Logan, Utah
Phone: (801) 756-4689
E-mail: jamiebennion@hotmail.com

BLOCK STARTS

Skill	Cue	Why?
Initial Block Setting	Front block 2-foot lengths from start line	Strongest position from which to push
	Back block 3-foot lengths from start line	
"On Your Mark" [Figure 16.1]	Hands on the track, behind the start line	
	Toes barely in contact with the track	
	Hands bridge on fingerpads; form a "checkmark"	Raises center of gravity
	Hands directly under shoulders or a bit wider	For stability
	Weight forward on the fingerpads	Engages forward momentum
	Head and neck relaxed, eyes looking 2 to 3 feet down the track	

Weight forward on hands

Hands bridge on finger pads, form a check mark

Hands directly under shoulders

Figure 16.1   "On Your Mark"

STARTS

Skill	Cue	Why?
"Set" (Figure 16.2)	Raise hips so the front leg is at 90 degrees, and the back leg is at 120 degrees	Optimal pushing position
	Weight forward on fingerpads	Engages forward momentum
	Shoulders directly over hands	
	Head and neck relaxed, eyes looking 2 to 3 feet down the track	
Gun (Figure 16.3)	Push hard with both feet	Stronger than pushing with just one foot
	Shoulders, head, hips are a pillar	
	Arms in opposition	
	Back foot steps with toe directly under hip	Creates a pushing action, rather than a pulling action
	Apply proper acceleration techniques	

Raise hips

Head and neck relaxed, eyes looking 2–3 feet down the track

Shoulders directly over hands

Figure 16.2   "Set"

Arms in
opposition

Shoulders, head,
and hips are a pillar

Push hard with both
feet

Figure 16.3   Gun

HURDLES

Skill	Cue	Why?
Approach	Eight steps to first hurdle	Move hurdles in so students can feel what eight steps (7 to 9 meters) is like. Practice running through the hurdle. Everybody can have fun and be successful.
Lead Leg	The foot that is back when you start will be your lead leg Lead with knee	Provides quicker leg snap into and off of the hurdle
Trial Leg	Bring knee to armpit Pull heel into hip Maintain flexed foot position Toe up	Shortens the lever for quicker recovery
Rhythm	1, 2, 3, hurdle; 1, 2, 3, hurdle	Eight steps to first hurdle and three steps between the hurdles = four contacts with the ground Maintain the same lead leg throughout the whole race
(Figure 16.4)	Sprint through the hurdles	Remember, hurdling is a sprinting event, not a running and jumping event

Lead leg—lead with your knee

Sprint through the hurdle

Figure 16.4　Sprint through the Hurdle

STANDING LONG JUMP		
Skill	**Cue**	**Why?**
Stance	Stand with feet shoulder-width apart	This creates a good base of support and optimal position for push-off
Swing Motion	In one smooth motion, bend knees to a sit-down position (90-degree angle)	The swing action creates momentum for optimal distance
	Raise arms behind body to shoulder height	
	Thrust arms above head in an aggressive forward fashion as you jump	
In Air	Stretch body as tall as possible, reaching for the sky	Uses vertical and horizontal velocities to increase distance
	Pull heels under hips and reach feet in front of you	
Landing	Land with heels stretched out in front of you	To avoid falling backward
	Pull heels under hips	
	Reach hands out in front of you	

RUNNING LONG JUMP

Skill	Cue	Why?
Approach	Take 10 to 12 running steps	Gives speed to jump farther
	Last two steps are like a basketball lay-up	Prepares you for the jump
Takeoff	Hit the board with one foot	Rule
In Air	Jump up and out	More power
	Arms above head and behind shoulders	More power
	Arch back like a C	More efficient in the air
	Close jackknife	Greater distance
Landing	Collapse buttocks to heel Collapse knees	
	Arms thrust forward	
	Feet together	

TRIPLE JUMP

Skill	Cue	Why?
Foot and Leg Action	Hop on one foot as far as you can go, landing on the same foot	See Chapter 5 regarding why and to get more cues on sprinting
	Take a long step with the opposite foot	Rules
	Jump off of that foot as far as you can for distance. Example: right, right, left, together	
	Land with both feet	
	Make sure to swing your arms upward and forward on the jump	
	Think: "hop, step, jump"	

RELAY		
Skill	**Cue**	**Why?**
Blind Handoff, Underhand		This pass is great because the runner keeps the arms driving in correct form
Receiver Arm Position (Figure 16.5)	"Slam the door directly behind you"	
	Make a checkmark with hand	Better target surface
Hand Position	Steady hand	Bigger surface area for baton to go in
Passer Arm Position	Focus eyes on hand	Watching the receivers hand helps put baton in the hand
	Hit the palm with underhand delivery	
Relay Drill (Figure 16.6)	Have a one-syllable cue: "hit" or "go"	Notifies the runner when to put the hand back. Good timing.
Exchange	Passer yells, "Hit"	Runner can hear
	First passer right to receiver's left hand	Won't drop baton
	Second passer left to receiver's right hand	
	Third passer right to receiver's left hand	
	Fourth passer left to receivers right hand	
	Keep baton in one hand only to help minimize dropping the baton	

Receiver—slam the door behind you, make a checkmark with hand

Steady hand

Passer yells "hit"

Hit receiver's palm with underhand delivery

Figure 16.5   Relay Hand Position

Passer yells "hit"

Baton exchange is in an alternating hand pattern

Figure 16.6   Relay Passer Code Drill

Chapter 17

Ultimate Frisbee

Ultimate Frisbee, born in Maplewood, New Jersey, in 1968, is a fast-paced, noncontact, and highly energetic sport. "Ultimate" combines elements from soccer, football, and basketball. The sport is unique that while it is highly competitive, there are no referees. The basis of Ultimate is a concept that originated with the sport itself: "Spirit of the Game." This concept allows players to focus on high performance rather than on officiating the game. Spirit of the Game also promotes integrity and fair play among all players of the sport.

Ultimate is a team sport in which one person alone cannot be the hero. Because of the fast-paced nature of the game, teammates must learn to communicate with each other about offensive goals, defensive strategies, and weaknesses within the team during play in order to score consistently.

Ultimate Frisbee is gaining popularity around the world, and with good reason. Although the sport has many challenging skills which take a lot of practice to master, it is a fun and rewarding pastime for all ages (Figures 17.1, 17.2)

Figure 17.1   All Ages Can Play

SKILLS LISTED WITH CUES

The cues in this chapter pertain to the following skills: backhand throw, forehand throw (sidearm), pancake catch, offensive movement, and defensive marking.

Figure 17.2   Rewarding Pastime

EQUIPMENT TIPS

1. Lots of Frisbees (discs) (Figure 17.3)
2. Colored vests
3. Scoreboard (play by set points, not time)
4. Rubber cleats (if available)
5. Cones with which to mark the fields

TEACHING IDEAS

1. Encourage the students to call their own violations. This is one of the few games in which players call their own violations. Students can develop integrity in game situations.
2. Modify the rules to fit the skill level of your class. Change the size of the playing field, number of steps, and so on.

Frisbee  Rubber cleated shoes

Figure 17.3   Equipment

3. Games are played to point value, not time. Decide a score to play to at the beginning of the game and play to that score. Examples of point game: 7, 11,13, 19 points. Playing to 11 points is the most common point game in Ultimate.

TEACHING PROGRESSIONS

1. Have the students practice throwing and catching. Let them find their own personal space, and give them plenty of room.
2. Side-to-side partner throws: One partner throws, one partner receives. The receiver starts in the middle. The thrower chooses which side to throw the disc to. The receiver moves to the side and catches the disc and throws it back to partner. The thrower throws to both sides. This keeps the receiver moving from side to side. When the partners have mastered this drill, add a defender.
3. Ready, Aim, Fire: Each student has a Frisbee. Line up all the students an arm's length apart on a field. Quickly check their grips and stances. Review the cues. Say, "Ready, aim, fire." The students run and get their disc, get in a line, and get ready to throw back across the field.

MINI-GAMES

1. Throwbee (see Chapter 8 for game rules)
2. Philadelphia Football (see Chapter 8 for game rules)
3. Play mini-games of 4 on 4, 5 on 5, and 6 on 6, on any flat, open space, with a fairly well marked end zone.
4. Frisbee Golf: Set up several golf courses. Determine par for each hole. Use hoops, buckets, and the like, as targets. Maximize participation by dividing your class into small groups.
5. The Game: Rules of Ultimate Frisbee
   The game is started with a team standing on each endline. The "pull," whereby the disc is thrown to the other team, begins the point. Players move the disc down the field by throwing it to each other. If the disc hits the ground or goes out of bounds, the other team gains possession. Once a player catches the disc in the end zone, a point is scored and the opposing team must walk to the far goal line and await the pull from the scoring team. The disc may never be handed off. It must always be thrown.
   - The player in possession of the disc must establish a pivot foot. The player cannot run with disc.
   - The disc may be thrown in any direction.
   - Double teaming is not allowed.
   - The defensive team gains possession whenever the offensive team's pass is incomplete, intercepted, or goes out of bounds.
   - Out-of-bounds plays turn possession over to the opposing team at the point where the disc went out of bounds.
   - No hand slapping to knock the disc down or out of the hand of the passer is allowed.

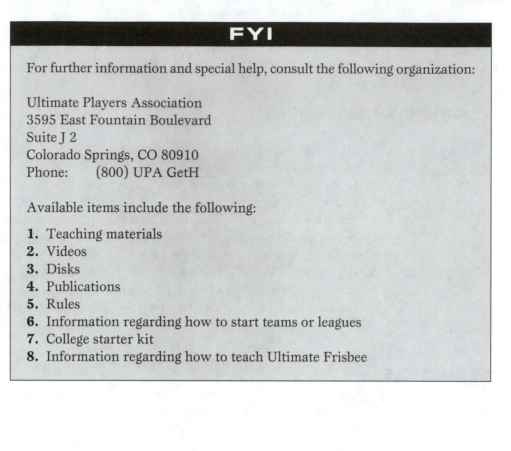

FYI

For further information and special help, consult the following organization:

Ultimate Players Association
3595 East Fountain Boulevard
Suite J 2
Colorado Springs, CO 80910
Phone: (800) UPA GetH

Available items include the following:

1. Teaching materials
2. Videos
3. Disks
4. Publications
5. Rules
6. Information regarding how to start teams or leagues
7. College starter kit
8. Information regarding how to teach Ultimate Frisbee

THROWING

Skill	Cue	Why?
Backhand Throw (Figure 17.4)		
Grip (Figure 17.5)	Pinch disc's edge with thumb and forefinger Three fingers hold inside edge	To control the flight of the disc
Stance	Stand sideways	Creates more power for distance
Throwing Action (Figure 17.6)	Backhand: wipe the table, disc flat Pivot, windup, step, snap, release	Disc will go farther Power on the disc
Index Finger Action (Figure 17.7)	Release like snapping a towel Point finger at target after follow-through Step toward target Elbow Wrist Finger Flick snap Point finger to target	Accuracy and specific target on which to focus

Pinch disc edge with thumb and forefinger

Figure 17.4   Backhand Grip

Three fingers hold inside edge

Figure 17.5   Backhand Grip

THROWING

Skill	Cue	Why?
Forehand Throw (Sidearm)	Form "V" with index and middle finger	
Grip (Figures 17.8 and 17.9)	Middle finger is pivot finger	To generate a spinning disc
	Roll off middle finger	
	Thumb holds outside edge of disc	
Stance (Figure 17.10)	Step same side	Smoother action
	Outside rim of disc lower than inside	Keeps disc flat while in the air
	Step (with leg on same side of throwing arm), snap wrist	Throw farther
Arm Action (Figure 17.11)	Elbow on hip, wrist snap	Strength comes from wrist snap
	Try not to use arm for strength on this toss. All wrist action.	

Stand sideways

"Wipe the table," disk flat

Figure 17.6   Backhand Throw (Stance)

Release like "snapping a towel"

Step toward target

Pivot, windup, step, snap, release

Figure 17.7   Backhand Throw (Release)

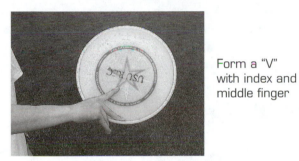

Form a "V" with index and middle finger

Figure 17.8   Forehand Grip (Top)

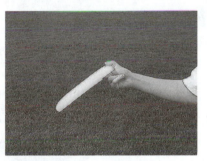

Thumb holds outside edge of disc

Figure 17.9   Forehand Grip (Side)

Elbow on hip

Snap wrist

Outside rim of disc lower than inside rim of disc

Figure 17.10   Forehand Stance

Snap wrist

Step with leg on same side of throwing arm

Figure 17.11   Forehand Throw

PANCAKE CATCH (TWO HANDS)

Skill	Cue	Why?
	Big hands	More surface area to hold on to frisbee
	Spread fingers	
Eyes	Watch disc all the way into hands	Keeps eyes focused on target
Hand Action (Figure 17.12)	Pancake catch: one hand on top of disc. One hand underneath disc.	More surface area on the disc for better control
	Make your hands be "Jaws"	Big hands, bigger surface to hang onto the disc

One hand on top, one hand on bottom of disc like a "pancake"

Big hands, spread fingers

Make your hands be "Jaws"

Figure 17.12   Pancake Catch

OFFENSE		
Skill	**Cue**	**Why?**
Receiver Options	Cut, circle away, cut, circle away. Keep moving!	Avoids same speed movements
	Fake and cut toward disc	Keeps the defensive players guessing
	Look while pivoting, fake, pivot, fake, anticipate!	The goal is to get open
	Get into position so you can receive a pass	
Thrower	Lead teammate with throw	Better option to catch the disc
	Throw to area, not to person	

DEFENSE		
Skill	**Cue**	**Why?**
Marking of Player with Disc (Figure 17.13)	"Stick like glue"	Not letting an opposing player get open for a throw
	Watch midsection	
	Keep hands low	
	Count to 10 slowly. Even count to 10.	Thrower has only 10 seconds to throw the disc before a violation is called
Marking with Receivers in the Field (Figure 17.14)	Stay between player you are guarding and the thrower	Intercept the disc or block the disc
	Watch both the disc and your opponent	
	Point one hand at opponent and the other hand at the player who has the disc	Watching the player you are guarding and the player who has the disc helps you anticipate where you should move
	Pistol action	

Defender watches opponent's midsection

"Stick like glue"

Defender keeps hands low

Figure 17.13   Defensive Marking of Player with Disc

Defender (middle) points one hand at opponent with disc and other hand at opponent without disc

Stand between opponents

Figure 17.14   Defensive Marking with Receivers in Field

Chapter 18

Volleyball

Volleyball is an excellent sport for all ages to play. It takes quick thinking, fast movements, and teamwork to be successful. This sport can be enjoyed by those ranging from the lowest skill level to the highest, especially with just a few modifications by different levels. People like to do things at which they succeed, and volleyball fits the bill for providing many opportunities for success during matches. It also doesn't discriminate against size, as the smaller individuals can be great defensive players in the back row, and the taller ones are good at the net. And if either can jump and is quick, that person can play at any position.

Volleyball teaches players how to stay focused and how to work with many people in a small area. It has a great capacity to teach players the principle of learning from their mistakes, and then forgetting them so that they can concentrate on the next play. After all, it isn't the mistake that matters, it is what players do afterward that counts—what a great life lesson this is! Volleyball provides many opportunities to practice this and other principles. Now, all that is necessary to make this happen is for you to teach correct skills and attitude.

This chapter helps you with skill progressions and modifications that allow younger players to find and enjoy success. Specific cues, coupled with simplified drills and games, are included to teach skills correctly.

SKILLS LISTED WITH CUES

This chapter presents cues for the following skills: forearm pass, overhead pass, underhand and overhead serves, offensive hit, spiking, and blocking.

EQUIPMENT TIPS

One of the most overlooked factors in playing and enjoying volleyball, and probably the most important, is the type of ball itself. If a rubber or hard ball is used, it is painful to hit. Younger players will be afraid to underhand pass or set the ball. Using good-quality volleyballs is a priority. Top of the line brand names are Tachikaras, Badens, or Mikasas.

If there is too little money to purchase better quality balls, check with the high school coaches and see if they have any older balls that your program could purchase at a discounted rate. Each year, gradually add a few good balls to your collection until you have an inventory of 15 to 20 to use. In the meantime, purchasing a few less expensive "soft-touch" balls will help you get by until you can afford enough of the better quality balls.

Another important factor in ensuring success for younger players in elementary schools is to lower the net. Adjusting the height of the net appropriately enables players to have more success in spiking, blocking, and serving. Hence, more players will attempt those skills as the probability of success rises. Most standard net systems are adjustable.

Other equipment that you should have on hand for drills and games:

- Three to four antennas per net (the extras are used to divide the court in half or into thirds)
- Ball cart that will hold 20 to 30 balls
- Flip chart
- Stopwatch
- Whistle
- Markers or cones

TEACHING IDEAS

1. You need to have high expectations of your students. Modified high school drills work wonderfully if the players are given the opportunity to experience many touches on the ball. For example, move the players closer to the net to increase the possibility of their success in serving overhand.
2. Play many 3-on-3 games. This increases the number of times a player touches the ball. Increased touches leads to more experience, which leads to more control. Control in volleyball is the key to success.
3. Because volleyball is a rebound sport, it is important that the players understand that the "ball knows angles." Where it goes depends on the angle of the players' arms.
4. In addition, if they understand that "simple is better than complex," they decrease wasted and unwanted motion. In the extremely quick game of volleyball, extra and excessive motion not only is wasted, but also is a detriment to the success of the sport. An example of this involves the underhand pass. Instead of "simply" coming straight up from the knees with a flat, straight platform (arms) to meet the ball, many players unnecessarily start

with the arms high (around the waist), dip them down as the ball comes, then bring them back up to hit it (called *pumping*). Or many young players start with their hands together and under their chins (as if they are praying), then take their hands down and up to hit the ball. This extra motion slows the players' defensive ability and interferes with their accuracy, depending on the speed of the ball. Cut out wasted motion—simplify.

5. Use local high school teams to demonstrate the correct skills to your younger players. It is very important that skill development provide a correct image for your players to imitate. If they have an idea of their goal, they are more apt to reach it. It is a fact that students who have watched their older siblings play a specific sport learn that sport more quickly and have more success at it. It isn't necessarily "in the genes," but in their experiences and observations.

6. During the first few days of teaching this game to beginners, do not overdo the underhand pass. It takes a week or two to "toughen up" their arms, and if you have them perform too many repetitions too early, their arms will be sore and it will be painful for them to hit the ball.

7. Set up opportunities for success. Make sure you challenge your players so they will always be extending themselves, but give them attainable goals. Reward improvement. For example, give them a number of good hits to reach in a row.

8. Have them work in groups of threes to increase their ability to angle the ball.

9. You should stay out of the drills as much as possible. You don't need the practice, they do. Your job is to give them immediate feedback. Catch those doing the skill correctly and praise them. This technique goes much further than constant correction. All players will be willing to receive praise and will have a positive image to copy. Try to give more praise than correction.

10. Always give your players the desired skill correction, instead of the negative. For example:
    - The desired teaching cue: "Keep your arms straight to pass."
    - The undesired teaching cue: "Don't bend your arms."

The first response leaves a positive image and goal. The second leaves a negative image and a reprimand.

SKILL PROGRESSIONS

1. Forearm pass
2. Overhead pass
3. Serving (both underhand and overhead)
4. Overhead hit
5. Spiking
6. Blocking

Teaching (skill) progressions are found at the end of each cue section.

MINI-GAMES

1. 2-on-2 games, half-court
2. 3-on-3 games, full court
3. 4-on-4 games with a designated setter
4. Queens/Kings Court
5. Scramble, and many other fun games, can be found in the book by McGown, Fronske, and Moser (see FYI section).

FYI

For volleyball coaches:

McGown, C., Fronske, H., & Moser, L. (2000). *Coaching volleyball! Building a winning team.* Boston: Allyn and Bacon.

FOREARM PASS

Skill	Cue	Why
Forearm Contact		
Hand Position (Figure 18.1)	Hands in front of knees	By placing your hands down by your knees, you are low and ready to come up and pass the ball when it comes to you
	Thumbs and wrists together	Makes a nice flat and strong surface for the ball to contact
Elbow Position	Elbows straight and flat	This provides a smooth surface to bounce the ball off straight
	Platform out early under the ball	No pumping action coming down and back. This wastes critical time.
Forearm Pass		
Foot Action (Figure 18.2)	Feet to the ball Beat the ball to the spot	Allows the player to be in the best position to contact the ball
	Shuffle	Faster way to get to the ball
	Face the ball; angle the arms Drop the shoulder	Helps the ball go where you want it to
Passing Action	Pass ball over lead leg	Better angle to setter
Focus of the Eyes	See the server; see the spin	Keeps your eyes on the ball and keeps you focused on a specific detail
	Focus intensely on the ball as it comes into the arms	Many balls will spin down or float to the side at the last second, and if the player does not watch the entire flight of the ball as it comes to meet his or her arms, it might not hit squarely on the arms

Thumbs and wrists together

Elbows straight and flat

Hands in front of knees

Figure 18.1   Forearm Pass (Hand Position)

Face the ball, angle the arms

Pass over the lead leg

"Platform" out early and under the ball

Figure 18.2   Forearm Pass (Foot Action)

Teaching Progression for Forearm Pass

1. Throw, Hit, Catch: A player tosses the ball to a partner, and the partner passes back (Figure 18.3). The ball is caught and tossed again. Repeat 10 times.
2. Toss, Pass, Pass: Two players start with a toss and keep passing back and forth until 20 passes have been tossed.
3. In a Line of Three: Player A passes to player B, who passes behind his or her head to player C, who passes long to player A. Rotate after 10 passes. Switch the person in the middle to give each player a chance to pass the ball backward over his or her head.
4. Triangle: Three players pass the ball in a triangle. This allows the passer to practice facing the ball and angling the arms. Switch after 12 passes.

Partner tosses ball, partner passes back

Figure 18.3   Forearm—Throw, Hit, Catch Drill

OVERHEAD PASS		
Skill	**Cue**	**Why?**
Ready Position (Figure 18.4)	Right foot forward	
	Face target	
	Square to the target	
	Big hands, curved hands around the ball	Big hands allow you to cover a wide surface area of the ball, which gives you more control and accuracy
	Shape early, hands up at hairline. Contact is made above hairline, thumbs pointing at each other.	Gives you more time to prepare to receive the ball
		This is a key for correct performance. Not shaping early is the biggest cause of failure of this skill. Overemphasize to your players to have their hands up extra-early.

OVERHEAD PASS

Skill	Cue	Why?
Arm Action (Figure 18.5)	Elbows out	
	Contact on fingerpads	Provides more surface area and more control
	Extend the arms Like a basketball chest pass, but at the ceiling	Full extension allows you to put the ball high and provides power. Also guides ball in right direction.

Contact made above hairline

Big hands, shape early

Elbows out, thumbs point at each other

Figure 18.4   Overhead Pass (Ready Position)

Elbows out

Contact on finger pads

Hands up at hairline

Figure 18.5   Overhead Pass (Arm Action)

Teaching Progressions for Overhead Pass

1. Throw, Hit, Catch: A player tosses the ball to a partner, and the partner passes back. The ball is caught and tossed again. Repeat 10 times.
2. Toss, Pass, Pass: Two players start with a toss and keep passing back and forth until 20 passes have been tossed.
3. In a Line of Three: Player A passes to player B, who passes behind his or head to player C, who passes long to player A. Rotate after 10 passes. Switch the person in the middle to give each player a chance to pass the ball backward over his or her head.
4. Triangle: Three players pass the ball in a triangle. This allows the passer to practice facing the ball. Switch direction of the pass after 12 passes.

UNDERHAND SERVE

Skill	Cue	Why?
Hand Position (Figure 18.6)	Palm up, make a big palm or Palm up, make a fist	Bigger surface area for ball to contact. Better control of ball.
Foot Position	Step toward net with foot opposite of throwing arm	More power to the ball
	Arm close to body, brush shorts	Better efficiency
	Arm straight	Helps with the follow-through
	Hit ball out of hand; follow-through toward target	Greater control of ball
Contact Ball	Contact ball on lower third of ball	
Nonhitting Arm	Extend ball in front of hitting arm	Decreases incidence of the ball going out of bounds to the player's left
Hitting Arm	Swing back to the height of the shoulder, like pitching horseshoes	Increases power

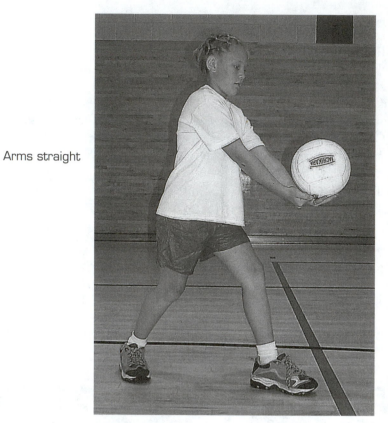

Arms straight

Make a big palm

Contact at lower third of ball

Figure 18.6   Underhand Serve

OVERHEAD SERVE (RIGHT HAND)

Skills	Cue	Why?
Ready Position (Figure 18.7)	Bow and arrow action	Keeps elbow high and ready to hit ball
	Stand sideways; left foot points at target	More power to serve the ball Weight transfer from back to front foot
	Hold ball in one hand	Simplifies the serve
	Ball in left hand and up in front of hitting shoulder	Eliminates extra movement and allows accurate and consistent contact with the ball
	Hitting elbow up	Timing to contact ball is more efficient
Toss (Figure 18.8)	Precise toss	Simplifies timing and decreases decision making

"Bow and Arrow" action of the arm, elbow up

Ball in front of hitting shoulder

Stand sideways, left foot points at target

Figure 18.7   Overhead Serve (Ready Position)

Precise toss

Step, toss, hit with heel of hand

Figure 18.8   Overhead Serve (Toss)

OVERHEAD SERVE (RIGHT HAND)

Skills	Cue	Why?
Hitting Action [Figure 18.9]	Step, toss, hit with heel of hand	Gives speed to the ball
	Swing to target Heel of hand to target	Directs power through the ball
	Like throwing a ball	
	Step under the ball and contact it high overhead	If the ball is contacted too far in front of a player, it has greater probability of going into the net. Stepping under the ball and reaching high makes the ball go higher, thus over the net.
	Reach high	
	Have a routine you do each time you serve, as with a free throw	Routines develop the same motor patterns for consistency

Teaching Progression for the Overhead Serve

1. Serve at the wall.
2. Serve from the attack line with a partner and move back.
3. Serve and chase the ball.
4. Serve to opponents, who try to catch the ball.
5. Serve in a game situation, 3-on-3 games, played on half-courts.

Reach high

Heel of hand to target

Like throwing a ball

Figure 18.9   Overhead Serve (Contact)

OFFENSIVE HIT

Skill	Cue	Why?
Used for Balls off of Net (Figure 18.10)	Elbow back, hand above head, rotate elbow forward, and reach up with an open hand	Rotation increases torque and equates into a faster, harder hit
	Hit ball at highest point of reach with the heel of the hand and follow through after contact at the intended target	Increases control of the direction of the ball
	Similar to a throwing action, with the hand above the head	
	Contact ball on bottom third	A higher contact increases the probability of the ball going over the net
	Watch the ball hit the hand	Decreases the probability of missing the ball. Increases the chance of a solid hit.
Hitting Action	Step under the ball, with the foot opposite of hitting arm	More power in the hit, and lining up the hitting arm with the ball is critical for the ball hitting the hand squarely or solidly
	The hitting arm should be lined up directly under the ball	

Hand above head

Watch the ball

Elbow back

Figure 18.10   Offensive Hit (Ready Position)

SPIKING (RIGHT-HANDED)

Skill	Cue	Why?
Hand Action	Fingers apart, hand open and firm	More control on the ball; able to snap, driving the ball down
Three-Step Approach	Step: Left-Right-Left Angular approach	
	Last two steps are more like a quick hop, with the left foot landing on the floor slightly after the right one	Simplifies the approach
	The arms start with the first step (go back)	Increases height of reach
	Left foot landing last tips the body at an angle	
	The body is turned toward the approaching ball	Increases torque of the body
		More power
Arms	Straight arms (both), start low (lower than waist), swing back on first step as far as possible, then back up on last step	Straight arms increase speed of swing, which increases height of jump and quickness of the hit
Bow and Arrow Action	Right elbow rotates back, keeping hand above head, then moves forward similar to a whip cracking, with the open hand contacting the ball in front of the body and fully extended	Increases power and speed of the hitting arm
		Hitting ball in front of right arm and body, ball will go down, not up or straight
Wrist Action	Snap wrist and follow-through toward the desired direction of the hit and then down	Controls the ball and puts spin on ball so it will go down into the court

Teaching Progressions for the Spike

1. *"You Go, I Throw"*: Players begin their approach and you toss the ball as if they have performed the proper approach. The players need to come to you. Toss the ball as they jump, a couple of feet from the net and directly in front of you.
2. *"I Throw, You Go"*: You toss the ball to the outside. The hitters start off the court and behind the line.

BLOCKING

Skill	Cue	Why?
Hands	Mickey Mouse ears Big hands Fingers spread wide Palms in front of face, facing the net	Ready position, no swinging hands Hands should remain in front of the body the entire blocking time. They never go directly above the blocker's head or behind it. Many times, the hands will come forward too late, thus trapping the ball between the blocker and the net.
Arms Extended	Directly up and over net Seal net between the hands and net Hold arms up there	Decreases possibility of ball being trapped between the blocker and the net No downward motion toward ball; less likely to hit net
Foot Action	Two steps moving to the right. Step with right foot; bring the left foot to over shoulder-length apart and jump. Stay loaded; bend knees and stay bent while moving to the ball, then go directly up without bending again	Simple and quick Quicker
Eyes	Look at hitter after ball leaves setter's hands and line up with her hitting arm	Better position to block ball and correct timing
Timing	Depends mainly on height of ball and the distance of the hitter from the net. The further away the hitter is from the net, the later the blocker jumps. The closer the hitter is to the net, the quicker the blocker jumps	

Teaching Progressions for the Block

1. Have players practice the two-step move with an opposing partner across the net.
2. Have blocking against hitters in the spiking drill. Be careful of spikers who run under the net. Blockers tend to come down on spikers' feet and sprain their ankles. Encourage setters to set the ball off the net (not tight). This decreases the possibility of injury.

Chapter 19

Cycling and BMX Riding

Imagine riding a bicycle over 2,300 miles but having only 21 days in which to do so. This is what elite cyclists, such as Lance Armstrong, encounter every July in the Tour de France. The sport of cycling grows continually. The mountain bike speed record on dirt has reached over 100 miles per hour.

Cycling is a sport that is easy to participate in, and children are learning to ride bicycles at younger and younger ages. Every child should have the opportunity to have her own bicycle and be taught the skills needed to ride it safely. More than ever before, children are learning these skills faster and easier. Every child learns at a different pace, but most children are free of the need for training wheels on their bikes by the age of 4 or 5. At this age, these skills are learned through trial and error. Because of this, proper equipment is critical.

SKILLS LISTED WITH CUES

The cues found in this chapter help teach proper techniques and skills needed for cycling, such as bike size, body position, pedaling, braking, cornering, riding uphill, riding downhill, riding in rough terrain, the bunny hop, BMX racing, riding curbs, partner peg riding, solo peg riding, and performing a wheelie.

EQUIPMENT TIPS

1. The most important piece of equipment is always the helmet. When purchasing a helmet, make sure that it is ANSI tested and fits properly. **Note:** Helmets come in child and age-specific sizes (Figure 19.1). Biking gloves are also a good idea.

Helmet

Gloves

Properly sized bike

Figure 19.1 Bike Equipment

2. When purchasing a bicycle, a wide variety of sizes will be available. Youth bicycles are found in 16-, 20-, and 24-inch wheel sizes. A bicycle mechanic will be able to fit the child to the proper wheel size and frame size.
3. Younger children should ride with coaster brakes rather than hand brakes, because of their low skill level.

BMX EQUIPMENT TIPS

1. BMX racing requires a full-faced helmet, long-sleeved shirt, and long pants.
2. Full-fingered riding gloves help with better handle grip, absorption of handlebar vibration, and protecting the hand if in a accident.
3. It is best to run foam padding on the stem, handlebars, and along the top tube of the BMX bike. This also helps with protection in case of accident.

TEACHING IDEAS

1. Statistics show that in the majority of bicycle accidents, the rider falls off the bike due to various reasons. The remainder of the accidents involve collisions with automobiles, fixed objects, or other cyclists.
2. Heavy emphasis should be placed on the proper use of crosswalks. When bicycling, children need to cross the street at crosswalks. And they should *walk* their bikes across, not ride them. This makes children more aware of traffic and more noticeable to drivers (Figure 19.2).
3. Children should ride their bicycles on sidewalks. This keeps them off the road and away from motorists.
4. Every bike, no matter how much it is ridden, needs a tune-up every year. If something is wrong with a bike, get it checked right away.
5. Discuss methods to keep the bike secure when is not being used (e.g., the purchase of a sturdy chain to attach the bike to a rack, if one is available) (Figure 19.3).

Walk bike across
a crosswalk

Figure 19.2   Crosswalk

Figure 19.3   Lock Bike

TEACHING PROGRESSIONS

The following skills should be taught in this order:

1. Find the correct bike size
2. Teach body position on the bike
3. Pedaling
4. Braking
5. Cornering.
6. Riding up hill
7. Riding downhill
8. Handling rough terrain
9. Curb and other obstacle riding
10. Traffic hand signals (Figure 19.4)
    - Left arm makes an upward vertical L: right turn
    - Left arm straight down: slow down, or coming to a stop
    - Left arm straight out to the side: left turn

Right signal   Slow down/stop   Left signal

Figure 19.4   Traffic Signals

MINI-GAMES

1. Riding around cones helps teach cornering and control on a bike. Set up cones far enough apart that turning will be simple and manageable. After the drill has been completed, move the cones closer together, allowing tighter turns and cornering. Continue this drill to teach precision.

2. Set up a bike course around the school to test skill levels. Include dirt sections with bumps, rocks, and other obstacles. This catches students' attention and makes riding more challenging and fun for them.

3. Cycling offers many competitive opportunities, including road racing, mountain bike racing, cyclo-crossing, track racing, and BMX racing. BMX racing is great for children who are looking for that competitive side to cycling. BMX racing is set up on a BMX track. It offers racing categories for different skill levels and age groups. BMX races include a series of qualifying heats (motos) in order to make it to the main moto. This is great, because children can race up to four times for one race. In the main moto, trophies, ribbons, and prizes can be won. After a child places so many times, he or she will be qualified for the next racing category. Note: Different BMX circuits have different classifications and qualifications. Refer to equipment tips for BMX racing.

FYI

For further information and special help, consult the following organization and source:

Bell Sports, Customer Service
1924 County Road 3000 North
Rantoul, IL 61866
Phone: (800) 456-Bell
Fax: (217) 893-9154

Bell Sports provides information regarding helmets:

1. Bell will replace your helmet, starting at only $20 if you write to it, explaining the crash.
2. With this information, Bell can do research on actual crashes.
3. A Bell helmet has many air vents, permitting hot air to be replaced by cool air while ridng. This ventilation reduces the risk of heat exhaustion.
4. A Bell helmet fits lower on the head and protects the occipital lobe of the brain, which is responsible for sight and other critical functions.

BIKE SIZE

Skills	Cues	Why?
Size	Good cockpit space	If space is too small, hunchback occurs
Upper Body	Seat to handlebar distance is comfortable	If space is too large, you end up in a stretched-out position, causing upper back and neck soreness
Legs	Stand over bar	
	Ride a few sizes	If the bike is too big, it will handle poorly, and you won't be able to react as fast when necessary
	Get smallest bike you are comfortable riding	Bike too big, high center, "ouch"
Seat Height	At bottom of stroke, knees slightly bent	It can cause hyperextension of the knees when the seat is too high. You also lose pedal efficiency.

BODY POSITION

Skill	Cue	Why?
Feet	Ball of foot over axle of pedal	Your power comes out of the ball of your foot, like when jumping
Seat Position	Position seat so that when knees and legs are at 3:00 and 9:00, seat is slightly behind ball of foot and pedal	This gives you optimum leg power out of every stroke
Upper Body	About 60% of body weight should be over rear wheel	Gives you more control of bike

PEDALING

Skill	Cue	Why?
Pedaling	Spin at a cadence of about 80 rpm Ride smarter, not harder	It's more energy efficient to spin more, rather than mash on the pedals
Pedaling Action	Spin pedal in circles, not squares Downstroke motion, like scraping mud off your shoes Backstroke motion, like picking up your feet	This maximizes power and pedal-stroke efficiency
Riding in a Straight Line	Keep eyes on road 10 to 15 yards ahead Ride straight	Helps prevent weaving as you ride

BRAKING		
Skill	**Cue**	**Why?**
To Stop Quickly (Figure 19.5)	Scoot buttocks back	Allows you to stop faster while maintaining good control
	Pedal at 3:00 and 9:00 positions	
	Squeeze both hand brakes evenly	
	Keep both wheels on the ground	Keeps tires from skidding
Shifting under a Load	Anticipate shift	
	Shift front gear first; fine-tune with smaller gears	Allows smoother and faster shifting
	Give pedals a hard push for a half stroke; then ease off and shift	

Squeeze both brakes evenly

Scoot buttocks back

Pedals at 3:00 and 9:00

Figure 19.5 Braking

CORNERING

Skill	Cue	Why?
Braking	Assess the speed and do all braking entering corner or curve	Applying brakes while leaning through a corner or curve causes handling problems
	Start wide and head for inner tip or point of turn	Not turning until well into the corner slows you down and can be dangerous
Anticipating Turn (Figure 19.6)	Visualize the line or path you will travel through the curve and follow it	Makes the turn faster and easier
	Body leans into the corner and carves your line through the turn	
	Keep outside pedal down; stand on it	Lowers center of gravity
Sharp Corner	Raise inside pedal to top of pedal stroke	Allows more distance between the pedal and the ground so there is less chance of dragging your pedal and crashing

Outside pedal down

Inside pedal up

Body leans into the corner

Figure 19.6   Cornering

UPHILL/DOWNHILL/ROUGH TERRAIN RIDING

Skill	Cues	Why?
Riding Uphill		
Sitting (Figure 19.7)	Balance weight 60% to 70% over back wheel and 30% to 40% over front wheel to keep traction in back	So you can keep good traction as you climb without the front wheel popping off the ground
	Shift weight to middle to keep front wheel down so that you do not lose traction in loose dirt	Makes you stronger when you ride because you are using your quads and hamstrings
	Pedal in circles, using both a pulling and pushing action on each pedal	
Standing Climb (Figure 19.8)	Stand, lean forward, push down on bars, and rock the bike	Gives you more power, rather than sitting
	Make sure your body and bike line stays straight	
Riding Downhill (Figure 19.9)	Shift weight back and down on seat	If you sit too far forward, you increase your chance of going over the handlebars
	Hold seat with upper thigh	
	Watch ahead; pick a path	
	Pedal is at 9:00 and 3:00	Won't hit rocks or other debris
Riding in Rough Terrain	Power through corner	If you shift and reverse, there will be more chance of wrecking
	Keep rear wheel behind you	
	Relax, go with the flow	
	Stutter-step; get dominant foot in front toe position	Allows your legs and arms to absorb the bumps, leaving you with more control of your bike
	Be like a shock absorber	
	Soak up the bumps with knees and arms, like a sponge	
	Let bike float over things	
	Straddle saddle; stand on pedals	
	Avoid hitting obstacles	

70 percent of body
weight over back
wheel

Use pushing and
pulling action on
pedals

Figure 19.7 Riding Up Hill (Sitting)

Body and bike line
stay straight

While standing, lean
forward, push down
on handlebars

Figure 19.8 Riding Up Hill (Standing)

Shift weight back
and down

Pedals at 3:00
and 9:00

Figure 19.9 Riding Downhill

THE BUNNY HOP

Skill	Cue	Why?
Riding in Rough Terrain (*cont'd*) To be used for jumping over large rocks, branches, and rocks in the trail	Go fast enough to maintain forward motion	So you can clear the object
	Stand up on pedals, with knees slightly bent	
	Just before reaching the object, bend knees and elbows so back is nearly parallel with ground	
	Pull up on the handlebars, as if you were riding a curb	
	When the wheel is in the air, push the handlebar out, forward, and down, as you leap or spring with your legs	Brings the back wheel up
	Your front wheel actually goes through an arc motion as you pull up on the handlebars, then push forward and down	

BMX RACING

Skill	Cues	Why?
Start	When starting gate drops, lift up front tire as you begin to pedal	Allows the racer to get over the gate faster, providing an edge over the competition
Turns, Embankments	Pedal through the turns and embankments when possible	Helps maintain momentum through corners
Strategy	Keep the rear wheel on the ground as much as possible	If the bike is always in the air, the racer loses valuable time and speed

RIDING UP/DOWN CURBS

Skill	Cue	Why?
Riding Down Curbs	Make sure speed is enough to maintain forward motion	
	Stand up on pedals, with both knees slightly bent	Helps to maintain control of bike
	Balance weight over pedals	
	Keep handlebars straight	
	Let front tire roll off curb and back wheel will follow	
	Slightly bend elbows and knees	Allows the body to absorb the shock of the bumps
Riding Up Curbs	Go fast enough to maintain forward motion	
	Stand up on the pedals	
	When you're about 3 to 6 inches from curb, pull up on handlebars to lift front wheel onto curb	
	When front wheel has landed, lean forward	Takes the weight off the back of the bike
	Continue to pedal through so that back tire just rides right up curb	

PARTNER/SOLO PEG RIDING—WHEELIES

Skill	Cue	Why?
Partner Peg Riding (Figure 19.10)	One partner stands on pegs	
	Put hands on other partner's shoulders	Balance
	Stand tall and hold on	Balance
Solo Peg Riding (Figure 19.11)	Arms straight	Balance
	Legs straight	
	Look up and focus on path	
Pop a Wheelie (Figure 19.12)	Pull handlebars up	Initiating more power
	Move weight back; lean forward	Balance
	Weight on lower pedal; hang on	

Back person stands tall
and puts hands on
partner's shoulders

Figure 19.10   Partner Peg Riding

Look up and
focus on path

Arms straight

Legs straight

Figure 19.11   Solo Peg Riding

Pull bars up

Move weight back

Weight on lower pedal

Figure 19.12   Popping a Wheelie

Chapter 20

In-Line Skating

In-line skating is an enjoyable new sport that can be introduced to people of all ages. Students from elementary, middle, and high schools can enjoy and learn about in-line skating. Many students already participate in in-line skating, and this activity can easily be added to any physical education class.

In-line skating can be incorporated into a physical education program under National Association for Sport and Physical Education (NASPE) Standards. Skate in School is a program developed by NASPE and Roller Blade, Inc., that comes with ready-to-use lesson plans and affordable equipment (skates, helmets, and protective gear).

SKILLS LISTED WITH CUES

Cues are presented for the following basic skills: standing up, ready position, falling, V-walk, using the ABT brake, striding, turning, use of edges, stopping, and swizzling.

EQUIPMENT TIPS

1. Each student *must* wear a helmet and knee, wrist, and elbow pads.
2. Organization of the equipment is very important.
   - Mark all of the equipment with permanent markers.
   - Mark skates with the size on the back of each skate. Skates should be stored as pairs on some type of shelving.
   - Mark all protective gear and helmets with S, M, L, or XL.
   - Keep equipment by type or by size. You can use large buckets, one each for knee pads, elbow pads, and wrist pads, or you can use mesh bags that hold one of each type of equipment, all the same size. Choose the method that works for you. You may want to experiment to find out which is better.

3. After each day's use, the equipment should be cleaned with a spray disinfectant and stored in a well-ventilated area to allow drying.
4. The first day of class should be used to go over rules and talk about the physical benefits of skating, the importance of protective gear, and the proper technique of getting and putting away the equipment.
5. Depending on the type of skates and brake pads, you can skate in the gym (with indoor skates) or on a flat, smooth surface outside. For indoor use, you need a nonmarking brake pad, like the ones Roller Blade, Inc., uses in its program.
6. All equipment should be maintained on a regular basis.

TEACHING IDEAS

1. Always discuss the importance of protective gear. Don't scare students, but remind them that a broken wrist or concussion is worse than a messed-up hairdo.
2. Talk to students about the physical benefits of in-line skating.
3. Discuss with students the importance of control. If control is maintained, falling should not occur very often. Each student's level of control may be different.
4. Students should be reminded to keep their body weight low and slightly forward, with knees bent, most of the time.
5. Discuss the skating area and use boundary markers and cones when possible. Also, establish traffic patterns for safety.
6. Start nervous beginners on floor mats to ease falls and build confidence.
7. Have students assist each other verbally, but not physically.

TEACHING PROGRESSION

1. Rules and procedures
2. Protective gear and skates
3. Standing up
4. Ready position
5. Falling
6. Stopping
7. Rolling and stopping
8. V-walk/stroking
9. V-walk, roll, and basic stop
10. Stride
11. ABT brake
12. Turns
13. Edges
14. Slalom
15. Forward swizzle
16. Backward swizzle.

MINI-GAMES

1. *Red Light, Green Light:* The goal of this activity is for students to practice stopping techniques.

2. *Musical Braking:* Students skate to music on a circular course. Periodically, the music is turned off for 3 to 5 seconds. The goal of the activity is that every student should come to a complete, controlled stop before the music is turned on again.

3. *Skating Pins:* Students skate in lanes up and down a flat area. A "wall" of bowling pins is placed at each end and a line is placed approximately 2 to 3 feet in front of the pins. The goal of the activity is that students perform the basic stop between the line and pins without knocking over any pins.

4. *Slalom Races:* Divide the class into teams of four. Set up a slalom course. In relay fashion, have the teams race through the slalom course, turn around the last cone, and race back to tag the next person in line. Every cone that is knocked down adds 1 second to the overall team score.

5. *Student Routines:* Put the students in groups of four to six. Have the students develop a skating routine to music of their choice. (Be sure the music is appropriate beforehand.) The students need to include at least four different skating skills in the routine. Have students present their routines to the class.

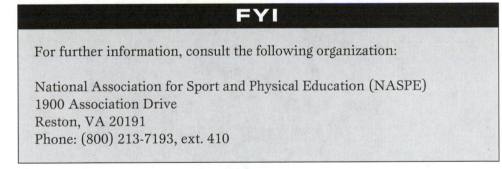

FYI

For further information, consult the following organization:

National Association for Sport and Physical Education (NASPE)
1900 Association Drive
Reston, VA 20191
Phone: (800) 213-7193, ext. 410

STANDING—READY POSITION

Skill	Cue	Why?
Standing Up	Start on both knees	Beginning skaters need to understand the most efficient way to get up, conserve energy, and not get frustrated
	Lift nonbrake knee and place wheels on ground	
	Place both hands on knees	
	Push up slowly	
	Position skates in a V (heels together)	
Ready Position (Figure 20.1)	Position skates in a V (heels together)	This position is needed to begin all movements
	Ankles, knees, and hips flexed	
	Weight forward and low	
	Arms forward and in front of knees	
	Put hands on knees to regain balance if falling backward	

Weight foward and low

Ankles, knees, and hips flexed

Position skates in a "V" position with heels together

Figure 20.1   Ready Position

FALLING—V-WALK—STOPPING

Skill	Cue	Why?
Falling (Figure 20.2)	Drop to all fours (knees, then hands, using plastic part of wrist guard)	Students need to understand that falling forward is the safest way to fall
V-Walk	Ready position	Basic step for movement. Students are in control of their speed.
	Shift weight from one foot to the other	
	While shifting weight, point toes out like a V	
Stopping #A Open ABT Brake	Weight on nonbrake leg	Do not lift toe in ABT. Keep all wheels on the ground.
	Put brake leg forward	
	Slightly lift toe	Great for beginners
	Press calf against back of skate	
	Shoulder and arms should be forward	

Use plastic parts of wrist guards

Drop to all fours— knees, then hands

Figure 20.2   Falling

FALLING—V-WALK—STOPPING

Skill	Cue	Why?
Stopping (*cont'd*)		
ABT Brake	Put weight on nonbrake leg	An effective means of stopping. Easy for students to have success.
	Slide brake foot forward	
	Press calf against cuff of boot and depress brake	
	Keep shoulders forward	
Standard Brake (Figure 20.3)	Scissor brake foot forward	
	Lift toe and press heel into the pad	
T-Stop Brake (Figure 20.4)	Glide and coast on both skates	Not all students have brakes
	Lift back braking foot and place behind front coasting foot in T position	Effective for more experienced skaters
	Apply pressure and ease skate to stop	

Lift toe, press heel
into brake pad

Scissor brake,
foot forward

Figure 20.3   Stopping Standard Brake

Lift back braking foot and
place behind front coasting
foot in T position

Figure 20.4   T-Stop Braking

STRIDING—TURNING—USE OF EDGES

Skill	Cue	Why?
Stride	Ready Position	Short strokes increase power
	V-walk	Don't twist body while gliding
	Right foot stroke, push forward; lift left foot off the ground, coast	
	Left foot stroke, push forward; lift right foot off the ground, coast	Keep nose, knees, and toes in forward position
	Repeat shifting weight back and forth	Take wide strides
	Note: There is minimal time that both skates are on the ground	Students experience smooth timing
Turns (For right turns; opposite for left turns)	Look to the right	Don't lean hips out. Rather, have upper body lean and leave hips aligned over skates
	Rotate upper body to right	
	Turn hips and knees to right	
	Skates about 6 inches apart	
	Lean to each side	
Use of Edges	One skate on outside edge	Allows smooth turning
	One skate on inside edge	
	Roll forward by pressing on edges	

TURNING AND SWIZZLING

Skill	Cue	Why?
Parallel Turn	Stride/coast, keeping feet under shoulders and parallel	Use with more experienced skaters
	Point shoulder to left; skates will follow, using one outside and one inside. Make the right leg lead with the outside edge	Students that feel comfortable on skates will experience success with these skills
	Lean into the outside edge	
Forward Swizzle	V position	These skills allow the students to move in multiple directions and combine a number of skills
	Bend knees, lean forward	
	Turn toes inward	
	Push heels out	
	Feet are about shoulder-width apart	
	Then bring feet together	
	Repeat	
Backward Swizzle	Same movement backward	
	Start with toes together (backward V)	
	Put pressure on the inside edge of both feet	
	Turne toes inward toward edge	
	Push heels out	
	Grab heels, pulling them back in (like gripping)	
	Bring feet together	
	Turn toes inward and lean	

BRAKING		
Skill	**Cue**	**Why?**
ABT Brake	Put weight on nonbrake leg	
	Slide brake foot forward	
	Press calf against cuff of boot and depress brake	
	Keep shoulders forward	
Standard Brake	Scissor brake foot forward	
	Lift toe and press heel into the pad	
	Heel into the pad	
T-Stop Brake	Glide and coast on both skates	
	Lift braking foot and place in back of coasting foot in T position	
	Apply pressure and ease skate to stop	

Chapter 21

Recreational Running

Why should children be encouraged to participate in recreational walking, jogging, and running activities at school? A teacher who includes running in her curriculum related the following student responses: "I can go hunting with my dad and keep up," "I can go on long walks with my mom," "I feel better when I go to class," "I can think clearer and work is easier," "I am losing weight," "I feel better about who I am," "Running keeps my mind on positive things," and "I perform better in other sports, such as basketball and soccer."

Recreational running is an activity in which the whole family can participate. A good pair of running shoes and comfortable clothing are all the equipment needed for one to venture into the great outdoors. Running and walking programs can bring families together. More time can be spent with parents, brothers, sisters, and neighbors.

Encourage all the children in your class to run or walk, not just the fast or fit ones. Run or walk with students who are slower and having a harder time. Network with them during this time and tell them you appreciate their effort. Let them know they are important. Just spending a few minutes with them conveys the message that you care.

Don't burn your students out! Keep their interest high by providing fun activities. The goal is to provide a fun experience and teach a lifetime skill.

In this chapter we provide strategies for 1-mile and 5-K fun-runs. However, it is important that the participants have a good cardiovascular fitness base and demonstrate their understanding of pacing before attempting these activities. We see many children start out too fast and subsequently "run out of gas" along the way.

SKILLS LISTED WITH CUES

In this chapter, cues are structured for the following: runners' cues, uphill and downhill running, building strider, pre-race routines, start of a race, racing strategies, and cool-down.

EQUIPMENT TIPS

1. A good pair of running shoes (Figure 21.1). Make sure the shoes are comfortable. For students who do not have the means to purchase shoes, you could have extra shoes available. You can elicit help from sporting goods' stores, go to a Goodwill store and purchase shoes, write a grant, or have people in the community donate shoes.
2. Each student should be encouraged to bring his or her own water bottle.
3. Clothing should be breathable.
4. Students should wear layers of clothing during cold weather.
5. Students should wear sunscreen and a hat on a hot, sunny day.
6. Popsicles or oranges are a nice treat after a fun-run (Figure 21.2).

TEACHING IDEAS

1. Teachers sometimes get too caught up in the mechanics of running. If teachers would block out the upper body and see what students' legs are doing, they often would find that the runners have good mechanics from the waist down. The runners are doing what feels good to them. Remember that the runners are propelled along the ground by the legs, not the arms, head, or hands. Arms are for balance. A reason why runners may not have perfect mechanics might be a leg length discrepancy, spine curvature, or individual structure differences. People are wired differently. The more students run,

Good pair of comfortable running shoes

Water bottles

Figure 21.1   Running Shoes and Hydration

Popsicles are a nice treat after a run

Figure 21.2 Treats

the more they will develop an efficient and economical running style. Relaxation and running economy are the keys.

2. Have your runners hydrate well before, during, and after jogs, runs, and races.

3. It has been suggested that a side ache can be related to weak conditioning, weak abdominals, shallow breathing, a large meal before exercise, and dehydration or excessive exercise intensity. Pain may be relieved by holding the arm over the head and stretching the side. This condition is not serious, just uncomfortable to the runner (Strand, Scantling, & Johnson, 1997).

4. A very important concept in running is that of pacing. In general, pacing means being able to run at a steady pace for a given length of time. Beginning runners have a tendency to start off too fast when given a certain distance to run. In a short period of time they are walking because they are not able to maintain the speed and move into an anaerobic state. Teachers need to teach pacing and let students experience what it feels like to run at a steady state for various intensity levels for various lengths of time (Strand, Scantling, & Johnson, 1997).

5. Incorporate homework on a monthly basis. Have students walk/jog or run for 20 minutes outside of class. Parents sign a form verifying that it was done. Award prizes to participants each month.

6. 2,000 Ways to Move Your Body! Have students bring in pictures of ways they stay in shape and put them on a big poster board (Figure 21.3).

TEACHING PROGRESSIONS

1. Start students with a 5-minute walk or jog inside; build up to jogging for 5 minutes.

2. When outside, the student's perception of distance changes. Have the students jog for 2 minutes, walk for 2 minutes, and build up to 5 minutes.

3. Run one lap outside, or a quarter-mile run. Build up to a half mile, to three-fourths of a mile, and to 1 mile.

Figure 21.3   2,000 Ways to Move Your Body

MINI-GAMES

1. *Pack Running:* Everyone stays with a group.
2. *Pacing:* Inform students how far they ran in 2 minutes.
3. *Orienteering:* integrates compass work with running
4. *Scavenger Hunt:* Have students run to get various items on a list.
5. *Run for Time:* Individuals try to "Beat your time."
6. *Cooperative Laps:* The class counts how many laps they ran in a specified time. The object is to increase the class lap score each time they run.
7. Enter or host a local fun-run (5-K run or 1-mile walk/jog).
8. *Class times:* Add each student's time for 1 mile. Add times up for a total class time. Try to beat the total time of other classes.
9. Plan a "Wellness Wednesday" or "Fitness Friday" before or after school. Have parents come and participate in a fun-run with their children.
10. *Fun-runs:* 5-K or less. Mileage for students:
    Grades K–5: 1 mile
    Grades 6–8: 2 to 3 miles

FYI

Kirkpatrick, B., & Birnbaum, B. (1997). *Lesson from the Heart.*
Human Kinetics Champaign, IL. (ISBN 0-880111983-7)
Phone: (800) 747-4457

Strand, B., Reeder, S., Scantling E., & Johnson, M. (1997). *Fitness education: Teaching concept-based fitness in schools.* Scottsdale, AZ: Gorsuch
Scarisbrick.

RUNNERS' CUES

Skill	Cue	Why?

Relaxation	Relax:
	    Face
	    Jaw
	    Neck
	    Shoulders
	    Arms
	    Hands
	
	Work on drills to stress these key areas
		Conserves energy, smoother running technique

Breathing	Belly breathing	Avoids side aches caused by breathing too fast and high in chest
	Pouch stomach out as you breathe in	Side aches also caused by starting too fast when not trained to do so

HILL RUNNING

Skill	Cue	Why?
Uphill	Short, quick strides	Prevents overstriding
	Compact stride, contained within oneself	
	Run on forefoot	
	Some forward lean, depending on steepness of hill	
	Maintain the hill; power over the crest	Prevents slowing down at the top of the hill and losing momentum
	Quickly get feet back to touching ground	Faster
Downhill		
Steep Hill	You must brake Use heel-first running stride	To avoid falling due to gaining too much speed
	Shorter braking stride	
	Arms come out further away	For balance
	Power down the hill on shorter, steeper hills	Prevents falling
Gradual Hills	Get body perpendicular to hill	
	Keep hips forward	
	Your arms swing out away from body for balance	
	Get foot under center of gravity	More efficient running technique
	Let gravity work with you	
	Keep body balanced	

BUILDING STRIDER

Skill	Cue	Why?
Used for Warm-Up (Practice/Races)		Warm up for the race Get the muscles ready to race
Distance	Total distance, 20 to 50 yards	
First 20 yards	Start from jog; go into a good pace by 20 yards	
Between 20 and 40 yards	Between 20 and 40 yards, accelerate to 80% full speed	
40–50 yards	Smooth transition to acceleration and then to deceleration	

RACING

Skills	Cue	Why?
Pre-race Performance Routines		
When to Warm Up	10–20 minutes before competition	Provides you enough time to be ready physically and mentally
Warm-Up	Jogging, dynamic stretches, and building striders	Muscles are warmed up, ready to go. This type of warm-up does not make the runner tired for the race
Hot Days	A shorter warm-up is needed	
	Be sure to hydrate well all day	Keeps body in top performance
	Warm up in shade, if possible	Prevents energy loss
Cold Days	A longer warm-up is needed	Gets the muscles ready to go
	Don't forget to hydrate	
Start		
Arm Position	Both arms down	
Leg Position	Dominant leg back	More powerful start
	Most weight on back foot	
Foot Action	Push off back foot first	Faster start, legs will be in correct running stride
Arm Action	Arms come up	To protect yourself at the crowded start
Strategy		
Beginning of Race	Quick start to get ahead of other runners	Gives you a jump start
	However, don't go out too fast for too long	The runner becomes tired too quickly
For Younger Children	Emphasize the importance of pacing	So you do not run "out of gas"
Positive Strokes	Control breathing Tell yourself, "I feel strong. I have trained harder than anyone else. I deserve this race."	Running is a mental game Must have positive strokes

RACING

Skills	Cue	Why?
Racing Strategy (*cont'd*) (Figure 21.4, see page 266)	Catch someone and pass them	Provides a specific goal on which the runner focuses. Keeps the mind mentally alert.
	Don't get into "no man's land." Don't run alone. Stay with group.	Other runners motivate and support you for maximum potential. Less likely to give up.
Corners and Hill	Accelerate coming out of a turn, over a hill, or through trees	Discourages other runners
End of the Race	Catch someone and beat them	Provides a goal and something to focus on at the end of the race. Takes the attention off of being tired.
Finish Line	Run through the line	Better time A racer might pass you
Cool Down after Race		
Exercises	Flexibility exercises, static stretches	Blood is circulating in muscles to get a better stretch
Jogging	Jog, very easy running. Keep moving. No acceleration Jog on flat terrain It is crucial to work muscles and ligaments through a range of motion	A cool-down helps recovery. Gets rid of lactic acid wastes. Could injure legs by over-training tired muscles

Positive self-talk

Catch someone and pass them

Stay in a group for support

Figure 21.4   Strategy for a Race

Chapter 22

Swimming and Diving

Swimming is an activity that can create many wonderful memories through-out one's lifetime: staying afloat for the first time, or jumping off the board for the first time, or the first freestyle race, or perhaps playing water games in the community pool on a hot summer day. Swimming is a lifetime skill. The benefits are numerous and include a great cardiovascular workout, development of upper and lower body strength, relief of stress, and invigoration for the day's activities. It's a wonderful activity for the rehabilitation of injuries or to ease arthritis, and can provide exercise for senior citizens up into their 90s.

Your main responsibility, when teaching swimming, is safety and providing a comfortable environment for the student. If you plan to teach swimming, it would be helpful to take a Water Safety Instruction class offered by the American Red Cross. The class is about 5 to 6 weeks long. This would give you the foundation and credibility needed to teach swimming in your curriculum.

You need to teach basic swimming skills, strokes, and water games. Teaching students to swim at an early age could, in the future, save a life. In this chapter, we provide cues and teaching progressions for swimming skills, four basic swimming strokes, and a variety of fun water games.

SKILLS LISTED WITH CUES

This chapter provides cues for the following skills: entering the water, blowing bubbles, floating on front and back, orientation to deep water, prone float from standing position (front and back), gliding front and back, standing up, rhythmic breathing, kicks (front and back), arm action (front and back), combined stroke on front, turning over to front and back, retrieving an object, bobbing in the water to travel to safety, and glides with push-off (front and back).

Teaching cues for intermediate swimming skills include alternating arm action in the back crawl, reverse direction on front and back, deep-water bobbing, buoyancy and floating positions, rotary breathing, sculling on the back, dolphin kick, scissors kick, treading water, rotary kick, surface dives, front and back open turns, and swimming underwater. Instruction on diving from the deck includes kneeling, diving action, and compact, stride, and shallow-water dives. Swimming strokes include front crawl, backstroke, elementary backstroke, and sidestroke.

EQUIPMENT TIPS

1. Goggles help beginning swimmers enjoy the water, open their eyes under water, and prevent the eyes from burning when swimming.
2. Kickboards (Figure 22.1) are mandatory for teaching beginning swimming skills and strokes.
3. Diving rings
4. Mini-fins are recommended when teaching the front and back crawl. The fins help students get horizontal in the water and experience success faster (Figure 22.2).
5. Plastic 8-inch balls and four hula hoops for wet bases
6. Water-basketball nets and water polo balls
7. Volleyball nets and water polo balls

TEACHING IDEAS

1. Some students might have a fear of the water because of a prior bad experience. In this event, try to find out as much information as possible about their backgrounds. Be very patient and build a relationship with these students; students need to trust you. If they don't trust you, they will not try a new skill. It is as simple as that. If students don't want to try a skill because

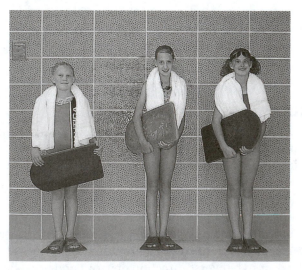

Goggles

Kickboards

Fins

Figure 22.1 Equipment

Figure 22.2 Use Kickboard and Fins to
Practice Swimming Strokes Progression

of fear, work with them at another time, perhaps before or after school. They may feel intimidated and embarrassed in a big class.

2. When teaching diving, be careful not to pressure students. Find another time to teach them. The extra time is worth it, because it usually only takes a few minutes to get them diving.

3. Work on the basics first. If a student has success with a basic swimming skill, such as a prone glide or a kneeling dive, she will gain confidence to move forward with other skills.

4. If you do not have a pool at your school, arrange to bus your students to a high school or community recreation pool, if this is feasible.

5. How do you organize a swimming class? First, have the class line up along the width of the pool. Place the best swimmers at the deep end and the beginners at the shallow end. Number off, 1-2-3. The 1s swim first, then the 2s, and then the 3s. This works on getting the students in shape. When they master this activity, have them swim the length of the pool.

TEACHING PROGRESSIONS

1. The fundamental skills in the cue sections are listed in a teaching progression.

2. Strokes to teach:
   Front crawl
   Back crawl
   Elementary backstroke (should be taught before the backstroke if a student has trouble floating on his back)
   Sidestroke

MINI-GAMES

1. Water basketball and/or water volleyball

2. Races sitting on kickboards, using the hands to propel. Race the width of pool.

3. Sharks and Minnows: a good game for working on staying underwater and being comfortable with the water. Most students love this game.

Rules

- One to four students are the sharks, and the rest of the class stands in the water against one wall.
- These students then swim underneath the water to the other side of pool.
- The sharks can tag them if they break the surface. Sharks can tag students only on their heads.
- When students get tagged, they join the sharks and try to tag the other students.

4. Water polo, played in the shallow end.

Rules

- Holding the ball under the water is not allowed.
- Players throw with one hand and catch with both hands.
- To start the game, have each team along opposite walls. The teacher throws the ball into the middle of the pool and students swim to the ball.
- Water polo can get violent, so stay on top of the game.
- Players cannot grab another swimmer and hold on, and they may not dunk another swimmer.
- The goal is to get the ball into the opponent's net.

5. Wet Base (modified game): A new water game, played like baseball.

Equipment

- One kickboard, used as the bat
- One light-weight 8-inch ball
- Four hula hoops, used for the bases
- Four 10-pound weights to keep hula hoops secure (optional)

Rules

- Two teams (four to 10 players per team)
- The batter stands in the shallow end of the pool, the pitcher pitches ball underhanded, the batter bats to deep end of pool. Allow no more than three pitches.
- The batter swims underwater through a hoop at first base, then to second, then to third, and then home. Score 1 point for making it back to home-plate.
- A ball that goes out on the deck is a foul ball.
- Outs are made just as in baseball.

FYI

American Red Cross. (1992). *Swimming and diving.* St. Louis: Mosby.

American Red Cross National Headquarters
430 17th Street Northwest
Washington, DC 20006
Phone: (202) 737-8300

SWIMMING SKILLS—BEGINNING

Skill	Cue	Why?
Entering the Water	Getting into a bathtub Splash arms, legs, face to get adjusted to water temperature	Gets children comfortable with the water
Bubble Blowing	Humming: like an alligator's face in water	Humming gets students blowing air out their noses most efficiently. Air exchange 80% through nose, 20% through mouth.
Supported Float on Front	Like being a hang-glider Chin up	Body is aerodynamic
Supported Float on Back	Like lying on sand, looking at sky Belly up	
Supported Kick on Front	Steamboat, or boil the water	
Supported Kick on Back	Boil the water	Keeps the feet at surface; less body drag
Holding Breath and Submerging Head	Be a submarine	
Orientation to Deep Water	Spider crawl on the wall Slide your hands Hug the wall Be a hinge	Helps you know where students are safetywise
Prone Float from Standing Position	Kick one leg up and then the other leg	

SWIMMING SKILLS—BEGINNING

Skill	Cue	Why?
Prone Float or Glide (Figure 22.3)	Superhero—be tall in water Superhero looking over the city Superhero looking for person in trouble Extend arms—point toes	The face must be in the water to have streamlined body position. If the head is up, the feet will sink.
Supine Float from Standing Position (Figure 22.4)	Head back, ears in water Push tummy to blue sky Kick one leg up and then the next leg	Aerodynamic in water Streamlined
Supine Float or Glide	Be a torpedo	
Prone Float to Standing Position	Lift head Make a cannonball; push arms down Stand up	Lifting head makes feet go to the bottom of the pool
Back Float to Standing Position	Tuck chin Cannonball Push feet and arms down Stand up	
Rhythmic Breathing (Figure 22.5)	Chin to shoulder Press ear in water Blow through nose and mouth. Exhale underwater. Keep blowing out of mouth as head comes out.	Mouth and nose out of water Prevents water going into the mouth
Flutter Kick on Front	Superman/Steamboat	

Face in the water

Extend the arms, point toes

Be tall in the water

Figure 22.3   Prone Float Guide

Head, ears
in water

Push tummy to
the sky

Body is
streamlined

Figure 22.4   Supine Float

Chin to shoulder

Press ear in water

Figure 22.5   Rhythmic Breathing

SWIMMING SKILLS—BEGINNING

Skill	Cue	Why?
Flutter Kick on Back	Straight legs Lie on sand; toes break water	Kick comes from the hips
Finning on Back	Hands like little wings	
Back Crawl (Arm Action)	Arms recover straight, like raising a hand to ask a question Graze ear/skim ear Pinkie finger enters water first	Keeps arms close to body More efficient
Pull Underwater	Make a question mark	Relieves strain on shoulder More efficient
Combined Stroke on Front	Reach over a barrel Point toes, like a diver	

SWIMMING SKILLS—BEGINNING

Skill	Cue	Why?
Turning over Front to Back	Drop one shoulder Roll like a log or hot dog	
Retrieving Object	Try doing a handstand in the water	
Bobbing in Water to Travel to Safe Area	Jack rabbit moves to wall Kangaroo moves to wall Blow out all bubbles. Take a breath when head surfaces.	Teaches control of breathing
Supine Glide with Push Off	Tuck position on wall; spring off wall like a torpedo Ears touch water	
Prone Glide with Push Off	One hand on top of the other; squeeze ears. Spring off wall. Superhero looking over city or looking for person in trouble Water level at crown of head	More efficient body alignment

SWIMMING SKILLS—INTERMEDIATE

Skill	Cue	Why?
Back Crawl (Alternating Arm Action)	One arm up, one arm down, graze ear Spin arms	
Reverse Direction on Front and Back	Pull harder with inside arm Make a U-turn Keep kicking to stay on top of water	
Deep-Water Bobbing	A frog leaping Exhale through nose; be like a rocket taking off	As you go down, arms push water over your head. As arms go up, they push water to your feet.
Buoyancy and Floating Position	Arms above head Fingers point to sky Knees bent Fill lungs with air	

SWIMMING SKILLS—INTERMEDIATE

Skill	Cue	Why?
Rotary Breathing	Hum in water	Air going out; water can't get in
	Bubbles through nose mostly	Allows the mouth and nose to come out of water
	Chin to shoulder	Head stays streamlined
Sculling on Back		
Flat Scull	Figure 8 motion, hands by hips. Palms in, palms out.	
Head First	Figure 8; fingers point to floor	
	Waving down	
Feet First	Figure 8; fingers point to floor	
	Waving up	
Dolphin Kick	Wave with body	Body motion crucial to effective dolphin kick
	Be a mermaid, with feet together	
Scissors Kick	Lying on side; ear in water	
	Scissors out, scissors in Up out together, glide	
	Cutting the water bring legs together	
	American splits	Student's leg movement must be along the surface of the water, not deep
Front Open Turn	Drop one shoulder, meet hands above head, streamlined	The swimmer cuts through the water faster, farther, and more efficiently
	Knees tuck against wall; submerge in water	You are loading the spring
	Spring off wall	
	Stay submerged	
Back Open Turn	Drop one shoulder, meet hands over head, streamlined	
	Spring off wall	
	Be a torpedo	

SWIMMING SKILLS—INTERMEDIATE

Skill	Cue	Why?
Swimming Underwater	Be a submarine	
	Scrape a big bowl with hands	More efficient pull
	Be a frog with the kick	
Treading Water	Look over fence. Keep head up.	
	Figure 8 with hands, palms up, palms down, or like spreading butter with sides of hands	
	Get wide in water	The wider you are, the better you float. More surface area, more buoyancy.
	Wide scissors kick or whip kick	
	Relaxed	Tight muscles make you sink
Rotary Kick	Sit on a horse, back straight	
	Get wide in water	The wider you are, the better you float. The more surface area, the more buoyant the swimmer is in the water.
	One foot rotates clockwise; the other foot, counterclockwise	
	Eggbeater	Power keeps your body erect
	Wax on! Wax off! (as in the *Karate Kid* movie) with your feet—same motion, just use the feet	

DIVING

Skill	Cue	Why?
Side-of-Pool Dives	All dives from the side of pool Water level at least 9 feet deep	Safety first
Kneeling Position (Figure 22.6)	Kneel on one knee, grip pool edge with other foot	If head is up, the student will flop in the water
	Head between arms, and fingers pointing toward water	
	Focus on target on bottom of water 4 feet out or on surface 1 or 2 feet from side	
	Tuck chin	
	Hold quarter to your chest with chin	
	Arms extended, squeeze ears	
Action of Dive	Lean forward; try to touch water	
	Push with front foot	
	Keep hips up, and dive over barrel	Keeps diver from falling into water
	Straighten legs	
	Push downward in water with hands	Breaks water with hands, not head. Does not hurt the head.

Arms extended, squeeze ears

Head between arms, tuck chin

Kneel on one knee

Figure 22.6 Kneeling Dive

DIVING

Skill	Cue	Why?
Side-of-Pool Dives (*cont'd*)		
Compact Dive (Figure 22.7)	One foot forward, one foot back	
	Kneel and rise	
	Head between arms; squeeze ears; point fingers at water	
	Hips up; stretch and touch surface of water	Reaching for water gets body into position to go head first
	Lose balance; push off toward water	Gets students going in head first
	Ankles together on water entry	
Stride Dive (Figure 22.8)	Stride stance	
	Front toes grab edge	
	Head between arms; tuck chin	
	Bend at the waist like breaking a pencil	
	Kick back leg up, hips up	Correct body angle for water entry
	Once body is underwater, point fingers to surface of water	
	Start kicking	

Head between arms, squeeze ears, point fingers at water

Hips up

One foot foward, one foot back

Figure 22.7   Compact Dive

Head between
arms, tuck chin

Kick back leg up

Stride stance

Figure 22.8   Stride Dive

DIVING		
Skill	**Cue**	**Why?**
Side-of-Pool Dives (*cont'd*)		
Long Shallow Dive	Push and stretch	
	Spear into the water	
	Over the barrel and through the hoop	
	Hands enter through doughnut hole	Helps divers dive out, not deep
	Go through the tunnel just below surface of water	

SWIMMING STROKES

Skill	Cue	Why?
Front Crawl		
Body Position	Be superhero	No wave drag to slow you down
	Be streamlined (like a racing rowboat)	
Head Position	Water level at crown	Best for streamlined body position
Arm Pull	S-pull thumb to middle of leg	More power
Arm Recovery	High elbow recovery	More energy efficient; no water drag
	Fingertip close to water	More energy efficient
Hand Entry	Spear a fish that is 2 to 3 inches below water. Reach.	Gets the arm in position for greater pull under the water
		More speed
Leg Action	Point toes like a diver's	Reduces wave drag, to swim faster. More streamlined.
	Boil the water	
	Straight legs kick from hips	
	Kick heels to surface	Less wave drag
Breathing	Follow the elbow back; look through window	Keeps body streamlined
	Roll chin to shoulder	Less wave drag
	Rotate body on skewer	Less drag
	Hum while face in water	More efficient air exchange
Backstroke		
Body Position	Streamline ears in the water	Less wave drag
	Eyes look at toes splashing water	
Hand Recovery (Figure 22.9)	Thumb leads coming out of the water, as if a string is pulling the thumb up	Specific goal for swimmer to heed
Shoulder Recovery	Raise hand to ask question	More efficient for best power position
	Straight arm; graze your ear with your arm	
Hand Entry	Pinkie finger always leads going into the water, palms facing away	Less splash

Thumb leads coming out of water

Graze ear with arm

Raise hand to ask question

Figure 22.9 Backstroke

SWIMMING STROKES

Skill	Cue	Why?
Arm Pull	Make a question mark with each pull	More power, less stress on shoulders
Leg Action	Point toes like a diver's Kick from hip	More streamlined. Move through the water faster.
	Kick toes to surface Make water boil	More power
Body Rotation	Rotate body on skewer Hip to sky	Keeps body streamlined. More efficient.
Elementary Backstroke		
Body Position	Ears in the water, arms down at side, streamline	Body is streamlined to move through water more efficiently
Arm Recovery	Tickle side with thumbs all the way to armpits	
	Elbow leads thumbs to armpits	
Arm Pull	Palm out; make a snow angel Make a T or airplane wings Soldier at attention	More power
Leg Action (Whip Kick)	Drop feet straight down	Requires less energy When knees come up, body sinks
	Try being knocked-knee	Gets legs in position for power phase
	Upper legs form a table Draw heels to buttocks; flex feet	
	Try drawing circles with your heels	Action phase more powerful
	Feet wider than knees	Action with feet faster More power

SWIMMING STROKES

Skill	Cue	Why?
Backstroke (*cont'd*)		
Coordination	Push feet, then squeeze	
	Point toes	
	Up out together, glide	Resting strokes give swimmer time to rest in the water
Sidestroke		
Body Position	Stay on side	Streamlined to move through the water more efficiently
	Lay head on arm	
	Lower ear in water	
Arm Pull	Tie a big knot	Best power from the arms
	Pick an apple from a tree and put it in your basket	Keeps upper body above the water
Arm Recovery	Rest the top hand on the top leg during the glide	More streamlined to move through water
Leg Action	Draw both heels to buttocks	Legs in best power position
	Up, out together	Less drag
	Do the split; step out, like walking	Power comes from here
	Top leg forward, back leg back	
	Legs do not pass each other when kick is finished	Keeps swimmer on side and streamlined
Coordination	Stay streamlined; count to 3 on glide	Rest
	Stay parallel with side	Maintains streamlined form. More efficient in the water.

Index

Appropriate touch, 6, 7
Armstrong, Lance, 233
Attention, getting, 13

Back crawl, 273, 274
Back float, 272
Back open turn, in swimming, 275
Backhand, Frisbee throwing, 211, 212
Backhand, tennis
    follow-through, 163
    grip, 155-156
    stroke, 162-164
    volley, 157, 158
Backhand passing, in hockey, 120
Backhand receiving, in hockey, 122
Backstroke, 280-281
    elementary, 281-282
Ball-carrying, in football, 134
Ball-handling
    in basketball, 106
    stationary, 93
Baseball pass, 98
Baserunning, 195-196
Basketball
    ball-handling, 106
    blocking, 110
    defense, 113-114
    equipment tips for, 91
    mini-games of, 92
    offensive footwork and moves, 111-112
    the pick, 111
    rebounding, 109
    shooting, 103-108, 109
    skills for, 93-114
    spacing in, 112
    teaching ideas and progressions for, 92
    water, 269

Batting, 193-195
Beach Ball Frenzy, mini-game, 35
Becoming a pillar, 61
skills and cues for, 63
Behind the back pass, 98
Bicycling. See Cycling
Blakemore, Connie, 8
Block starts, in track and field, 199-201
Blocking
    in basketball, 110
    in football, 134
    in volleyball, 231-232
BMX riding, 236
    equipment for, 234
    skills and cues for, 243
Body awareness, 61
Braking
    on bicycle, 239
    on in-line skates, 256
Breathing, in swimming, 271, 272
    rotary, 275
Building strider, 263
Bunny hop, on bicycle, 243
Buoyancy, 274

Cafeteria Quad Ball, mini-game, 142
Cardiac Bypass, mini-game, 141
Cardiac Court Quad Ball, mini-game, 142
Carnegie, Dale, 6, 7
Catcher, softball, 195
Catching
    of basketball, 96-100
    benchmarks for, 29-30
    equipment for, 30, 77
    of football, 87, 128, 129, 130, 131
    of Frisbee, 214
    ideas for teaching, 30

Catching (*cont.*)
  illustrated, 34, 84, 85
  mini-games for, 33, 35, 78-79
  in Quad Ball, 147-148
  skill progressions, 30-33, 35, 78, 84
  skills and cues for, 31, 83
  of softball, 190
  teaching ideas for, 78
Challenge, The, 6
Chest pass, 96, 97
Chipping, in soccer, 175
Circle formations, 12
Colors, learning, 28
Content standards, for physical education, 2
Converting to an aerial ball, 144-147
Cooperative laps, 260
Cornering, on bicycle, 240
Crab walk, 93
Credibility, gaining, 5-6
Criss cross rope jumping, 47
Cross-checking, in hockey, 117
Cues
  and analyzing skills, 14-15
  and assessing performance, 16
  and correcting technique, 15-16
  customizing, 8
  defined, 2
  effects on learning, 4
  getting, 4-8
  importance for students, 3
  importance for teachers, 3-4
  as motivators, 3
  nonverbal aspects of, 9
  and performance, 15
  tips on using, 4-5
  types of, 2
Curbs, and bicycling, 244
Cycling
  bike size for, 237
  body position for, 238
  braking, 239
  bunny hopping, 243
  cornering, 240
  downhill riding, 241, 242
  equipment for, 233-234
  mini-games for, 236
  partner peg riding, 244, 245
  pedaling, 238
  in rough terrain, 241
  safety issues, 235-236
  solo peg riding, 244, 245
  teaching ideas and progressions for, 234-235
  up and down curbs, 244
  uphill riding, 241, 242
  wheelies, 244, 246

Defense, in basketball, 113-114
Demonstrations, 13
Dewey, Thomas, 5
Disabled students, cues for, 14
Diving, 267
  equipment for, 268
  side-of-pool, 277-279
  teaching ideas and progressions for, 269
Dolphin kick, 275
Double Dutch rope jumping, 50
Double-foot rope jumping, 45
Downhill bicycle riding, 241, 242
Dribbling
  in basketball, 94-96
  in soccer, 173
Drop back, quarterback, 131
Dunking, basketball, 109
Dynamic stretching
  equipment tips for, 60
  mini-games for, 60
  skills and cues for, 62
  teaching ideas and progressions for, 60

Equipment, providing, 11-12

Falling, on in-line skates, 251
Feedback
  examples of, 6
  giving, 7-8
  importance of, 5
  negative, 7
Five misses, mini-game, 153-154
Floating, 271, 272, 274
Floor hockey
  equipment tips for, 115
  grips for, 118
  goaltending, 123-124
  mini-games of, 117
  passing and receiving in, 119-122
  rules of, 117
  shooting, 122-123
  skills for, 117-124
  stance for, 117-118
  stick handling in, 119
  teaching ideas and progressions for, 116-117
Flutter kick, 272, 273
Fly ball, fielding, 192
Follow-through, tennis, 161
Football
  ball-carrying, 134
  blocking in, 134
  equipment tips for, 125-126
  hand-offs, 133
  kicking, 129, 130
  mini-games of, 127

modified flag, 127
   quarterback skills, 131-132
   receiver skills, 135-136
   snapping, 130
   teaching ideas and progressions for, 126
   throwing and catching, 128-129, 130, 131, 312
Footwork, offensive, 111
Forearm pass, 221
   illustrated, 222
   teaching progression for, 223
Forehand, Frisbee throwing, 211, 213
Forehand, tennis
   follow-through, 161
   grip, 155
   stroke, 159-161
   volley, 156, 157
Forehand passing, in hockey, 119-120
Forehand receiving, in hockey, 121-122
Free throws, 107-108
Front crawl, 280
Front open turn, in swimming, 275
Fun-runs, 260

Galloping, 24
   skills and cues for, 58
Goalkeeping, soccer, 181-182
Goaltending, hockey, 123-124
Grips, tennis, 155-156
Ground ball, fielding, 191

Hand-offs, 133
Heading, in soccer, 179
Helmet, bicycle, 233
Help defense, in basketball, 114
High Knees, 73
High-sticking, in hockey, 117
Hills
   bicycling on, 241-242
   running on, 263
Hockey. *See* Floor hockey
Hopping, 23
   cues for, 57
Horizontal jumps, 56
Hurdling, 201-202

In-line skating
   braking, 256
   edge use in, 254
   equipment for, 247-248
   falling, 251
   mini-games for, 249
   standing, 250
   stopping, 251-252
   striding, 254
   teaching ideas and progression for, 248

turning, 254-255
   V-walk, 251
Infield ground ball, fielding, 191
Integrated activities, 14
Interference, in hockey, 117

Jackson, Phil, 6
James, William, 5
Jump shots, 108
Jumping, 23
   in basketball, 109
   double-foot, 45
   horizontal, 56
   single rope, 42, 44
   vertical, 56

Kicking
   mini-games for, 78-79
   punting, 90, 129, 130
   in Quad Ball, 148-149
   in rope jumping, 48
   skill progressions, 78
   in soccer, 178
   in swimming, 271, 272, 273, 275, 276
   teaching ideas for, 78
Kicking a stationary ball
   illustrated, 37
   mini-games for, 38
   skill progressions, 38
   skills and cues for, 36
KISS principle, 3, 4

Lateral passing, 132
Lay-ups, 105-106
Leaping, 22
   skills and cues for, 58
Locomotor Color Tag, mini-game, 28
Locomotor skills
   activities for, 27-28
   advanced cues for, 51-58
   equipment for, 20, 51
   ideas for teaching, 20
   mini-games for, 52
   teaching ideas and progressions for, 52
   types of, 20-27
Long jump
   running, 203
   standing, 202
Long-rope skills
   skills and cues for, 42
   teaching ideas and progressions for, 43

Man-to-man defense, in basketball, 114
Management skills, 10-12
Mini-games, 7

Mini-Volleyball Tennis, 79
Modified flag football, 127
Musical Braking, mini-game, 249

Negative feedback, 7
Nonverbal feedback, 6, 7

Obstacle course, 28
Offensive footwork, in basketball, 111
Offensive hit, in volleyball, 229
Offensive one-on-one moves, in basketball, 112
On-ball defense, in basketball, 113, 114
One-hand push pass, 99
One-on-one moves, offensive, 112
Orienteering, 260
Over the Net, mini-game, 35
Overhand serve, volleyball, 88, 226-228
Overhand throw, 31
    illustrated, 32
Overhead pass, 223-224
    illustrated, 224
    teaching progression for, 225
Overload, 4-5

Pacing, 259, 260
Pack running, 260
Pancake catch, of Frisbee, 214
Passing
    in basketball, 96-100
    in football, 128, 132
    in hockey, 119-120
    in soccer, 174, 176
    in volleyball, 221-226
Pawing action, 72-73
Pedaling, on bicycle, 238
Peg riding, 244, 245
Performance
    assessing, 16
    cues to strengthen, 15
Philadelphia Football, 79
Pick, the, 111
Pickle-Ball
    characteristics of, 151
    equipment for, 152
    mini-games for, 153-155
    scoring in, 167
    serves in, 167
    teaching ideas and progressions for, 152-153
Pillar exercises, 64-66
    illustrated, 71
    skills and cues for, 71
Pitching
    football, 132
    softball, 193
Posture, 53
Prone float, 272

Protocols, 10-12
Pulse-a-Fire Quad Ball, mini-game, 142
Punting, 90, 129, 130
Push pass, 99

Quad Ball
    ball handling in, 144-148
    court for, 138
    equipment tips for, 137-138
    mini-games of, 141-142
    rules in, 139-141
    safety guidelines for, 141
    scoring in, 139-140
    skills in, 148-150
    teaching ideas and progressions for, 138
Quarterback dropback, 131

Racing
    post-race cooldown, 265
    preparation for, 264
    starting, 264
    strategy for, 264-265, 266
Ready position, for in-line skating, 250
Rebounding, 109
Receiving
    in football, 135-136
    in hockey, 119-120
Red Light, Green Light, mini-game, 249
Relationships, building, 10
Relay races, 204-205
Respect, fostering, 9
Roosevelt, Theodore, 10
Rope jumping
    criss cross, 47
    Double Dutch, 50
    double-foot, 45
    equipment for, 40
    kicks in, 48
    mini-games for, 41
    single-foot, 46
    skills in, 39
    teaching ideas and progressions for, 40-41
    turning in, 49
Rotary kick, 276
Rough terrain, bicycling in, 241, 242
Running, 21
    building strider, 263
    cues for, 261
    equipment for, 258
    on hills, 262
    justifications for, 257
    mini-games for, 260
    reinforcement for, 258, 259
    skills and cues for, 55
    teaching ideas and progressions for, 258-259
    for time, 260

Running A's, 73
Running long jump, 203
Ryan's Ball, mini-game, 176-177

Scavenger hunts, 260
Scissor walk, 93
Scissors kick, 275
Serving, Pickle-Ball, 167
Serving, tennis, 165
    teaching progression for, 165-166
Serving, volleyball
    illustrated, 89
    overhand, 226-228
    overhand vs. underhand, 88
    underhand, 225-226
Set shot, 101-103
Sharks and minnows, mini-game, 270
Shooting, basketball
    dunking, 109
    free throw, 107-108
    fundamentals of, 103-105
    jump shot, 108
    lay-up, 105-106
    set shot, 101-103
Shooting, hockey, 122-123
Shooting, soccer, 178
Side-Court Quad Ball, mini-game, 142
Sidestroke, 282
Signals, for cyclists, 235, 236
Single-foot rope jumping, 46
Single-rope technique
    jumping, 44
    sizing, 44
    skills and cues for, 43
Skating. See In-line skating
Skating Pins, mini-game, 249
Skills
    analyzing, 14-15
    locomotor, 19-28, 51-58
    rope jumping, 39-50
    throwing, catching, and kicking, 29-38, 77-90
Skipping, 26-27
    skills and cues for, 57
Skipping A's, 73
Slalom Racing, mini-game, 249
Slashing, in hockey, 117
Sliding, 25-26
skills and cues for, 58
Slow-pitch softball. See Softball, slow-pitch
Smiling, 6
Snapping a ball, 130
Snowball Fight, mini-game, 33
Snowman tag, mini-game, 28
Soccer
    ball control in, 172
    chipping in, 175

dribbling in, 173
equipment for, 169-170
goalkeeping in, 181-182
heading in, 179
long passing in, 176
mini-games of, 170
offense in, 183
passing in, 174
shooting in, 178
teaching ideas and progressions for, 170
throw-ins in, 179-181
trapping in, 176-177
Soccer Croquet, 38
Soccer Golf, 38
Softball, slow-pitch
    baserunning in, 195-196
    batting in, 193-195
    catcher's job in, 195
    catching of, 190
    equipment for, 185-186
    fielding in, 191-192
    mini-games for, 187-188
    modified games of, 188
    pitching in, 193
    teaching ideas and progressions for, 186-186
    throwing of, 189
Softball Throwbee, mini-game, 176
Spacing, in basketball, 112
Speed Throw, mini-game, 78-90
Spiking, in volleyball, 230
Sprint accelerations, 74
Sprinting drills, 63, 75
    equipment tips for, 68
    importance of, 67-68
    mini-games for, 69
    on in-line skates, 250
    pillar concept and, 67
    progression of, 72-73
    schedule for, 69
    skills and cues for, 72
    teaching ideas and progressions for, 68-69
Standing, 53, 54
Standing long jump, 202
Start and stop signals, 10
Starts, in track and field, 199-201
Stationary ball-handling, for basketball, 93
Stick handling, 119
Stopping, on in-line skates, 251-253
Stretching. See Dynamic stretching
Striding, on in-line skates, 254
Striking
    activities for, 89
    illustrated, 89
    overhand serve as, 88
    underhand serve as, 88
Student Routines, mini-game, 249

Students
  getting cues, 4-8
  importance of cues to, 3
  opportunities to respond by, 5
Summitt, Pat, 6
Super Quad Ball, mini-game, 142
Supine float, 272, 273
Supportive climate
  developing, 8-9
  importance of, 9-10
Swimming, 267
  beginning skills for, 271-274
  equipment for, 268
  intermediate skills for, 274-278
  mini-games for, 269-270
  strokes for, 280-282
  teaching ideas and progressions for, 269
  underwater, 276
Swizzling, on in-line skates, 255

Tag, Snowman, 28
Target Practice, mini-game, 35
Teachers
  communication skills of, 5-6
  importance of cues to, 3-4
Teaching models, 13
Technique, correcting errors in, 15-16
Tennis
  characteristics of, 151
  equipment for, 152
  grips for, 155
  mini-games for, 153-155
  scoring of, 166
  strokes for, 159-164
  teaching ideas and progressions for, 152-153
  volleys in, 156-158
Three-Person Chase, mini-game, 198
Throw-ins, in soccer, 179-181
Throwbee, mini-game, 79
  softball, 176
Throwing
  benchmarks for, 29-30
  elbow action in, 82
  equipment for, 30, 77
  of football, 128, 129
  of Frisbee, 211-214
  "around-the-horn," 186-187
  ideas for teaching, 30
  illustrated, 32
  mini-games for, 33, 35, 78-79
  in Quad Ball, 148
  release point for, 82
  skill progressions, 30-33, 35, 78, 81
  skills and cues for, 33, 81
  of softball, 189
  teaching ideas for, 78

Throwing a football
  grip for, 86
  skills and cues for, 85
Toe kick, 36
  illustrated, 37
Track and field
  block starts in, 199-201
  equipment for, 197
  hurdling, 201-202
  jumping events, 202-203
  mini-games of, 198
  relay events, 204-205
  teaching ideas and progressions for, 198
Trapping, in soccer, 176-177
Traveling skills. *See* Locomotor skills
Treading water, 276
Triple jump, 203
Tripping, in hockey, 117
Turnaround, mini-game, 35
Turning
  on in-line skates, 254-255
  in rope jumping, 49
  in swimming, 275
Two-hand chest pass, 96, 97

Ultimate Frisbee
  defense in, 215, 216
  equipment for, 208
  history of, 207
  mini-games of, 209
  offense in, 215
  rules of, 209
  skills for, 211-216
  teaching ideas and progressions for, 208-209
Underhand serve, 88
  volleyball, 225-226
Unsportsmanlike conduct, in hockey, 117
Uphill bicycle riding, 241

V-walk, on in-line skates, 251
Verbal cues, 2
Vertical jumps, 56
Visual learning, 4
Volleyball
  blocking in, 231-232
  characteristics of, 217
  equipment for, 218
  mini-games of, 220
  offensive hit in, 229
  passing in 221-226
  serving in, 225-228
  spiking, 230
  teaching ideas and progressions for, 218-219
  water, 269
Volleys, tennis, 156-157

Waiting, minimizing, 12
Walking, 20, 54
  activities for, 53
  skills and cues for, 53
Walking A's, 73
Warming up, 40

building strider, 263
importance of, 59
  See also Dynamic stretching
Water polo, 270
Wheelies, 244, 246
Wooden, John, 6